8-27-56

Religious Living With Nursery Children

In Church and Home

PHOEBE M. ANDERSON

Published for the
Co-operative Publication Association

THE PILGRIM PRESS · BOSTON

To
Phil, Ross, Ray, and Amy
all of whom
have contributed more to
this book than they, or I,
will ever know.

Contents

THE CO-OPERATIVE SERIES
LEADERSHIP TRAINING TEXTS

Many thousands of lay workers in Protestant churches attend interdenominational leadership education schools each year. It is essential that the courses offered and the text materials used be acceptable to the many varieties of Protestant groups found in our American communities.

The Co-operative Series of leadership education textbooks are produced to meet that need. They are planned by the Division of Christian Education of the National Council of the Churches of Christ in the U. S. A., representing thirty-nine Protestant denominations. The Co-operative Publication Association, an interdenominational group of denominational editors and publishers, selects the writers and provides editorial supervision to insure sound educational values, practical usefulness, and interdenominational approval and acceptance.

Introduction

One minister asked another, "What do you do with parents of young children? Do you have meetings for them, or couples' clubs, or what? And if you have meetings, what kinds of programs do you have?"

A young mother spoke up at a class of the teacher training institute. "My husband and I are teachers for a three-year-old group in our church. What religious experiences and Christian ideas should we be teaching these children?"

Parents are asking on every hand, "If our child is really learning his first ideas of religion at home, when and how is he learning them, and what is he learning? We don't know. Will you, the church, help us?"

The churches today are providing facilities and various kinds of care for more young children than ever before. And with the children come endless questions — our questions. How should the nursery department be organized? What kinds of facilities must we have in order to set up a crib room? How can the church work with parents in the religious nurture of their children? Who should call on the families of nursery children and what good will come of it?

It is the purpose of this book to deal with these questions and others like them. The way a child becomes a mature Christian, methods by which teachers grow in their skill and understanding of children, some ways in which a church may work with the parents of young children, how the nursery department of a church should be set up and administered, the "why" and "how" of the church-sponsored weekday nursery school — all are discussed here as aspects of the work of the nursery department.

This book was written for all who are concerned with the religious growth of young children: parents, teachers, ministers, church school superintendents, nursery home visitors. It is the author's hope that whoever reads these pages with his mind alive and his heart aware will be persuaded that to learn to live wisely and skillfully with a child is, in truth, a Christian vocation. And the church that learns how to help parents live this way is performing a most effective and valuable ministry.

Whatever there is of wisdom in these pages I owe to those who taught me: first, to Dr. Ross Snyder. He has a deep sensitivity to the yearnings and the triumphs, the heartaches and the joys of a child, and of a seminary student. I learned from him that a child is "the most delightful object in the universe," and each day I discover that truth anew.

My other equally unassuming teachers have been the many children with whom I have lived and worked during the past ten years. First, those of the Salvation Army Day Nursery, behind the stockyards, in Chicago; second, those of the weekday nursery school of the Glenview Community Church, Glenview, Illinois; and third, those who have taught me most, both to my consternation and to my delight, my own Ross, Ray, and Amy.

I want to express my appreciation to Florence Schulz, my good friend and former colleague in the teaching and the administration of a church school program for three-year-olds, for the uncounted hours she spent typing manuscript, reading proof, and raising questions for further consideration; to Dr. Seward Hiltner, Professor of Pastoral Theology, the Federated Theological Faculty of the University of Chicago, and Robert Lipgar, both of whom carefully read chapters six and seven and made invaluable suggestions for their improvement; to Dr. Ross Snyder, Associate Professor of Religious Education at the Chicago Theological Seminary of the Federated Theological Faculty of the University of Chicago, and Martha Snyder who read the entire manuscript and shared with me their insights and their experiences at various points throughout the text; and to my editor, Grace Storms, who patiently led me through the complexities of organization, simplification, and grammar so that what I wrote could be understood.

But without the devotion of my husband, Phil, who gave much critical help, constant encouragement, and frequent assists with the responsibilities of our home, this book could never have been written. To him to whom I owe the most, I want to say " Thank you " sincerely, humbly, lovingly.

PHOEBE ANDERSON

Chicago, Illinois
February 20, 1956

PART ONE

Teaching Young Children

He destined us in love to be his sons through
Jesus Christ, according to the purpose of his will.

Ephesians 1: 5

CHAPTER ONE

Three-Year-Olds — How They Grow

On a Sunday Morning

IT WAS a beautiful fall Sunday morning. The children were coming all at once, and there was much busyness in the hall and around the door of the three-year-old room. Mrs. Todd watched and listened. Several tones lower than the high, happy voices of the children the parents could be heard, some relaxed, some anxious, some harried and annoyed.

"Where's your coat hook, Ronnie? Oh, this one with the dog picture."

"Don't lose your money, Alan. Better put it in the basket right away."

"Leslie! Come back here and take this hanky for that nose! No, I don't have time to lift you up to the fountain. You don't need a drink anyway."

"Be a good girl now, Betsy; play nicely with the children."

Standing a few feet away from the center of this mostly happy scene, looking — and probably feeling — like an "extra," not needed at the moment, was Katie. Alice Todd, the head teacher of the three-year-old group, felt the child's need to be included some place, by someone.

"Good morning, Katie. How are you this morning? Is that a pretty new dress you're wearing today?"

3

Katie nodded with a pleased look on her face and was murmuring "and I got new shoes, too" when Ronnie, who had just happened in on the conversation, made a perceptive but damaging remark.

"It looks 'way too big for her."

For a brief moment Mrs. Todd could not think of what to say. How to accept Ronnie, restore Katie's sense of "all rightness," and still deal with the fact? The dress was too large.

"Ronnie, I bet Katie's mommy had to buy a pretty big dress for Katie, so she could wear it to church school lots of Sundays instead of just a couple. Katie's growing so fast that she would not be able to wear that pretty dress for very long if it weren't a little bigger than she is."

Ronnie said "oh" and went after the sports car on the shelf above the blocks, which he really had had his eye on before the dress conversation diverted him. Katie smiled a quick smile and went to tidy up the dish cupboard in the housekeeping corner, a self-appointed, every-Sunday task.

Loud wails echoed from the hall. Mrs. Todd found Peter, just two, in his father's arms. Carol, his three-year-old sister, watched and listened anxiously. Their mother explained, "Peter wants to stay with Carol. He never leaves her side, but he isn't quite two and that isn't old enough for this group, is it?" When Mrs. Todd said no, Carol's parents bade her good-by and left quickly. Carol began to cry.

Mrs. Todd stooped and took Carol's two cold little hands in hers. "You don't need to cry, Carol. You know where your mommy and daddy went, and you know they'll be back when church is over, just like all the other mommies and daddies. You do understand that, don't you?"

Big tears lay full in Carol's blue eyes. "Then why did Peter get to go with them? Why didn't Peter stay here, too?"

"Oh, so that's the trouble. Let me tell you about that. You know, Peter really is not a big enough boy for our nursery group, so he went home with your daddy while your mother and you are at church. Peter can come when he is older, next year."

4

Mrs. Todd paused. Carol had listened intently, seemed *almost* convinced that it was all right. " She half wants to stay; she *needs* to stay for her own growing independence and sense of accomplishment," Mrs. Todd said to herself.

To Carol she said, " You know, I haven't had time to choose a picture to set up on our table. Will you come with me and help me choose the best one? " Carol took the proffered hand, and together they returned to the room.

In a few moments the picture was chosen, and Carol decided to do some ironing.

Jimmy was complaining. " Miss Alice, that boy's taking my puzzle." Mrs. Todd, known to the children as Miss Alice, found " that boy " a puzzle of his own and suggested they trade when each was finished. The boys neither accepted nor rejected this proposal, and Mrs. Todd went over to the work table. Miss Jane was putting some paste for each child in baby food jar lids, and Betsy was smacking colored scraps of paper on top of paste gobs in such considered — and apparently endless — succession that the creation was fast becoming three-dimensional. Mrs. Todd found herself feeling as pleased with the activity as Betsy seemed to be.

" I've got to tinkle," sounded from beside an array of blocks. It was Charles, who had not attended for some weeks. He had a new sister at home, and, understandably, the family schedule had been upset enough so Charles had missed several Sundays.

Mrs. Todd was wondering how he was finding life with a busy mother who spent lots of time with the baby and probably little time with him, when her mind came back quickly to the matter at hand. The " tinkle " had already been accomplished; Charles was soaked.

" Did your pants get wet already, Charles? That's too bad. I guess you didn't call me soon enough."

" I guess not. I just didn't know I was going to do it. It was done before I knew it. What will I do? Do I have to go home? " He was becoming tearful.

" No, Charles, you don't have to go home. I have extra under-

pants and overalls right here in my cupboard, and they'll fit you."
As she was helping Charles get into them she added, "All children
sometimes have accidents, and it doesn't really matter. We'll let
you wear the dry clothes home, and next Sunday you can bring
them back to us. How will that be?"

"Fine. I won't forget." As Charles returned to his blocks, he
almost knocked over Katie who was waiting with two others for
their turns in the bathroom and listening to the whole "wet
clothes" conversation.

"I had an accident once," confided Katie to Miss Alice.

"So did I."

"So did I and my mother was real mad. . . ."

Back in the room Carol had finished ironing and had put the
dolls to bed. She stood for a minute looking about and then
returned to Mrs. Todd's side and asked for a story. Mrs. Todd
took the picture Carol had chosen. It was of a boy being examined
with a stethoscope by a doctor. Together, she and several children
made up the story about the picture. The children were quite
eager to relate their own experiences with doctors, and the story
really became an excellent "telling time." Mrs. Todd said a
"Thank You" prayer for doctors that really grew out of the
feeling of the moment, and the next second Leslie wanted "her"
story. She had chosen a picture of Jesus and the children about
which Mrs. Todd then told. The attention being amazingly good,
she taught the children a song of church bells, which she had
planned to use if it seemed "right," and the children talked of the
bells in their church. There were even a few minutes spent
"seeing if we know each other's names" before the children returned to their play. Mrs. Todd made a mental note to think
about this period after she got home.

The morning was nearly over. Leslie and Shelley together built
a high tower, the first experience of working together for either
of them. Mrs. Todd "helped" so that neither child haplessly
knocked the tower over, lest the other child become so annoyed
that he or she would not try it again. Michael and Katie had two
disagreements over the dishes. "Katie kept taking my cups,"

6

Michael said. Mrs. Todd soothed the tempers, helped the cups get equally divided, and asked herself, " Why is this happening? " . . . also to be considered later.

Marcella turned over Jimmy's just-completed puzzle right at the moment when he was studying it with considerable satisfaction. He took a poke at her. She yelled. Miss Jane rushed from the work table, rebuking Marcella as she approached. " Oh, Marcella, you shouldn't have done that! " Children looked up from their play in every corner of the room, and Alice Todd made another mental note, this time for the next teachers' meeting. " How do teachers learn to live with and respond to children with a calm and easy manner and a light touch? "

" Miss Alice, look at my picture." Henry held up a colorful paper-and-paste picture.

" It's very nice, Henry. Do you want to take it home? "

Henry was already at his coat hook, taking down his coat. Mrs. Todd looked at her watch. It was not quite time for the parents to come. " Henry, why don't you put your picture on the wide window ledge here, and I'll read you some stories until it's time to go home. You'll get too warm if you put your coat on now; your mother is still in church."

Henry did not want to. He was finished for the day. He had played happily and created a satisfying picture. Now he wanted to take that picture to his mother and go home — immediately. Mrs. Todd said she knew that he had finished his morning and that he could go as soon as his mother had finished hers. Henry stood right by his coat looking through the open door as Mrs. Todd began to read a story to a few children seated on the rug. Miss Jane and Miss Harriet were quietly helping the rest of the children to finish their activities and put things away. One by one these children joined the group on the rug until all but Jimmy and Marcella were there. They spent the rest of the morning working puzzles.

Henry slowly edged back into the group and at the end of the story, which was about how people and animals grow, he announced, " Today, I'm going to do some growing."

"I'm sure you are, Henry. In fact, I think you're doing it right now."

The door at the end of the hall opened, and there were the mothers and daddies coming from the church service.

What Three-Year-Olds Are Like

Careful observation of a group of three-year-olds for an hour on Sunday morning reveals not only a great deal about this age in general; but it also is the best way to come to know one child in particular. By observing a group of children we can see the wide variations in motor skills, intellectual understanding, emotional maturity, social awareness, and development of religious personality. We also can see, over a period of time, the specific development in these areas of any particular child. As teachers, we need to know our children. Yet we often find ourselves so busy with the program for the day that we fail to observe the children with keenness and understanding.

Let us look for a moment at some of the characteristics of three-year-old children, both as a group and as individuals, that Alice Todd observed and pondered over as she wrote of the children in her journal.

"The general tone of happiness in the hall indicates that the children enjoy the church experience and are glad to be here again. I suppose three-year-olds generally enjoy being with other three-year-olds even if they actually do very little together. I wonder what 'church' means to each of these children? To Ronnie is it a sports car; to Katie, a dish cupboard that always needs putting in order; to Carol, a picture file; to Leslie and Shelley, smooth building blocks; to Charles, dry clothes? These are the things the children might tell their parents about their church. But I think their happy feelings on the inside spring from experiences they can't tell about. The words would be too hard to find, words for feeling glad about growing into a too-big dress, feeling secure and able to be alone without mother, discovering that it's fun to do things with other children, feeling relieved to find that 'accidents' are acceptable.

8

"Almost every child can recognize 'his' picture identifying the hook for his clothes and can remember it from week to week. What other things can a child remember for a week? Songs? Stories? Or must he be personally involved in the experience in order to remember it . . . like planting the seed himself instead of hearing about seeds. In my teaching, am I counting too much on what the children *remember* as a measure of what they learn?

"What ideas do the children have about money and its importance? . . . I'm thinking about Mrs. Ray's remark to Alan not to lose his money. Should I be doing something with the money the children bring besides turning it over to the church school treasurer? What should it be?

"There is considerable difference among nursery children in how they enter a group. Katie and Carol needed emotional support; Ronnie probably knew he was going to play with the sports car as soon as he entered the door; Jimmy began in the quiet part of the room where the books and puzzles were. Are these children growing in their feeling of security in the group? How much time does Katie spend in her little corner by the dish cupboard? What else does Ronnie do besides run his favorite car? What are the other children doing? *I must pay more attention.*

"These children grow fast. Katie's too-big dress and Betsy's too-short one betray the same characteristic. They have heard about how big they are growing, which probably accounts for the interest in the growing story and for Henry's remark at the end. I wonder if any of the children is concerned about how big he or she is?

"Much of the play is a clear imitation of the adult activity which they see and understand. Most of this play centers around the mother's activity at home. With what part of their fathers' lives can — or do — these boys identify? Do they play men's roles from firsthand experience or from make-believe and story material? They knew some things about the doctor. What do they know of 'office daddies,' or 'factory-working daddies'?

"There is great variation in physical skill. No one can color within an outline; only two can cut. The children enjoy pasting and clay activities. These have a nice squishy feel, but no one has yet intended any design with paste except Henry. His creation this morning was purposeful, a thing to be shared and treasured. Some children can manipulate puzzle pieces into the right places, some

9

can't; some can build towers and balance blocks, some can't; some can dress the dolls — even fasten the snaps, some cannot.

"In singing and rhythms there also is considerable difference. Some children can carry a tune, march in time, jump, hop, or gallop to a tune. Most cannot do these things. . . . I think we will give our scissors to the kindergarten; they are frustrating to most of these children. . . . Could we devise any more large muscle activity? We need more.

"Is the nursery group so stimulating and exciting an experience that the children have to be toileted more often than usual? I wonder if Charles' accidents are frequent and how they are treated at home. I must go to see Charles — not just his new baby sister. I'll call Mrs. Kent for an appointment, let her know that I plan to devote most of the time to Charles, and why. Wonder how she feels Charles is getting along at this point. She may need help.

"There are several indications of intellectual ability: skill with puzzles; imagination that can devise a story; attention span that sometimes stretches to fifteen minutes in a group activity; ability to understand concepts like growing. What sense of time do these children have? They can understand, 'in a few minutes,' and, 'after the story is over.' How do they understand tomorrow, and the next week, and next Sunday, or last Sunday? And long ago when Jesus lived?

"There was much learning about human relationships this morning. Katie learned that taking Michael's cups made Michael object. I hope she also learned that the teacher will help children straighten things out. Come to think of it, Katie and Michael are the smallest ones in the group. Was Katie, in the 'too-big' dress, trying to build up her own self-esteem by 'picking on' Michael? . . . Through her experience this morning Marcella should have learned to ask for Jimmy's puzzle instead of taking it. Did she learn that through Miss Jane's 'teaching,' or did she merely feel adult disapproval without a very clear understanding of why or of how Jimmy felt or of the rights of others? . . . Leslie and Shelley learned that building blocks together is fun.

"Did the children today find the teachers helpful to them in what the children wanted to do, understanding of their difficulties before they understood them themselves, always ready to treat them as persons, allowing them to make their own decisions, choose their own activity, create their own picture or block play or housekeeping situation, hang up their own clothes?"

It is easy to see from these few observations of a Sunday morning session that the usual way of describing nursery children in terms of their *physical, emotional, social,* and *intellectual* development doesn't wholly describe a child. None of these concepts of development is a separate entity that can be untangled from the others, brushed off, laid bare, and measured like the mercury column on a thermometer. They are descriptive terms, not definitive or exact ones, and a child grows in all these ways at the same time, and in more, too. *Psychological* and *religious* growth are two other aspects of growth just as impossible to measure, but equally valuable as descriptive terms.

Take Carol, for example. We may know that she is 39 inches tall and weighs 41 pounds, has just learned to ride her " trike," and seems to prefer her left hand. Emotionally, she seems not very happy and cries loud and long at the slightest scratch or unintentional bump. Socially, she seems fearful of extending herself to anyone, teacher or fellow pupils. She plays alone most of the time. She seems bright, can accurately count from four to six objects, works new puzzles quickly, knows all the colors including light and dark shades, asks endless questions of the teacher all the time.

But when Carol comes hesitantly into the nursery room in her nylon organdy dress and patent leather shoes, bedecked with locket, bracelet, and gold baby ring, and says to you, " My daddy isn't working today and he came to church with us," you find that none of the information you have does you much good. You know lots of things about Carol, but you do not know Carol. For she is the complex sum or whole of all you have observed, plus every experience she has had, every person she has dealt with, and every interpretation she has given to those experiences and persons in her long three and one-quarter years. No one will ever completely know Carol, for she is unique in all the world. But for a teacher to appreciate just this much about a child, his uniqueness, there is none other like him, is to take the road to discovering that every Carol and every Henry is perfectly delightful, a person to be treasured, cared for, and understood.

Yes, Carol is more than the sum of all the facts we can garner about her. We need to know this "more." What is going on inside the brown-eyed lass in the perky organdy walking slowly into the room? What kind of person does she think she is? What kind of place is she discovering the church to be? What kind of persons has she decided her teachers and the other children are? Unless we can discover at least partial answers to these questions, we cannot effectively establish a personal (therefore, a teaching) relationship with her.

The Developmental Task — The Clue to Effective Teaching

What is going on inside Carol? What is the big thing in her life that she needs to get done?

What is this for you — for me?

Each of us is a person of particular motivations and yearnings that underlie all that we say and do, that make us unique, different from everyone else. There is a great struggle going on inside each of us, and lots of lesser struggles, too: to possess something we have wanted for a long time; to master a new skill; to complete a training course; to attain certain educational goals; to get along with one's superiors (or spouse); to succeed at a new job; to become a better mother; to find a faith that will hold life together.

Our lives are organized around tasks such as these. We are purposeful creatures who act in terms of values we hold, seeking to acquire or accomplish some goal we see before us. The person whose life is not organized around some such intentional activity feels useless, unwanted, lost. Such a person seems to have lost his "aliveness," he is weary, energy-less; he does not want nor is he able to "get into the swim" of life about him. He is ill and needs help.

Children, like adults, have a great deal of similar unfinished business before them: to learn to ride their "trike"; to do the things of which their parents approve; to understand and get along with adults; to be able to do the things the other children do; to establish their right to make decisions; to have ideas; to become independent; to find out what the world is like — light switches, angleworms, muddy puddles, icicles, and snow. The list is endless, and the items are not mutually exclusive. Any child can have a considerable hidden agenda of things to be done, worlds to be explored and conquered, people to be understood, problems to be worked out.

This " unfinished business " or " struggle going on " has more accurately been called " developmental task." For each child there is a unique task, a job-to-be-done, that concerns no one else as it does him. This task arises from three sources, usually working together: one, the child's body develops and his muscles must do new things; two, he himself chooses (often unconsciously) to accomplish the task; three, society (his parents, or friends or teacher, or all other people) expects him to accomplish the task. If the child successfully completes his developmental task, he is happy and is able to move on to others. If he does not complete it, he is unhappy, feels social disapproval, and often has difficulty with the tasks that arise at a later age. As the phrase implies, the specific nature of the developmental task changes with age, growth, and development; but developmental tasks are characteristic of all human life, be it preschool, adolescent, or old age.

For an example at the nursery level, let us look at Carol's behavior on Sunday morning.

First, she is three and one-quarter years of age, sturdy, physically competent, able to keep up with a group of nursery children. Second, she wants to belong to the group. Her mother reported that Carol could hardly wait for Sundays to come around so she could get her pretty clothes on and go to church school. Third, her parents and the teacher expected her to join the group happily, without tears or fears.

One of Carol's developmental tasks, therefore, is to be able to get along happily with a group of almost strangers without feeling fearful, lost, deserted, or inadequate. Physically, she is ready to do it; by personal choice she *wants* to do it; the people important to her *expect* her to do it.

On this particular Sunday morning Carol, with the teacher's help, took another step along the road of accomplishing this task. If Carol continues to get along happily in the nursery without her mother, she will be free to face other tasks involving her growing independence from her mother, and she will probably succeed in accomplishing them. If she fails here, the next time she faces this task — perhaps at kindergarten — she will come to the situation with feelings of inadequacy and anxiety that will make the task even harder. She may accomplish physical separation from her mother and never achieve emotional independence. Such is the new wife who leaves her husband for her mother after the first quarrel.

Understanding this concept of the developmental task, which each child has on his hands, is most important for *all* teachers. For only if we are wise enough to understand the clues the child gives as to the nature of his task, and skilled enough to provide whatever help the child needs at the moment for accomplishing the task, have we truly, and in the most real sense, become his teacher.

The child will then have the thrilling experience of being understood by one who helps him accomplish something he wants very much to do. Consequently, this experience will become the basis for mutual trust and love between the child and you, his teacher. Having once been understood, the child can then forgive you when you fail to understand. And, amazingly enough, the trust and love and forgiveness he experiences in relation to you, his first teacher and frequently the first adult he comes to know well outside the family, become the attitudes with which he meets and extends himself to all other people. This is the way love is learned: " We love, because he first loved us."

Some developmental tasks, such as learning to put on one's clothes, are relatively easy, and once mastered they pretty much stay mastered. Others are more difficult, and are achieved by degrees over a long period of time, even a lifetime, such as learning

14

to be a sensitive, responsible member of the family of man. Most of us dress ourselves with little thought about how to do it. Few, if any of us, are able always to live and work and act with concern and sensitivity toward our fellows, even with considerable thought.

Children of nursery age all have some developmental tasks in common; but the clues any child gives about himself and his concerns, and the methods he uses to achieve what he needs to do, are uniquely his own. Our job as teachers is to read the clues aright and to help the child in his struggle to achieve — as Mrs. Todd did for Carol. The child's growing edges are at this point of his developmental tasks. Here is where learning takes place — personal, vital, important learning. Here is where the nursery leader becomes the child's teacher as well as his friend, for how the child feels about himself after he has struggled with his concern is what he has learned.

For example, suppose Carol had not been ready to stay without her mother. Suppose that Mrs. Todd with all her skill had not been able to help her feel secure and wanted in the three-year-old group. What would Carol have learned? No one, of course, can say definitely. Carol may have learned, " The nursery is a place with nice toys and a nice teacher where mothers leave their children. If you don't want to stay, the teacher will find your mother and she will take you home."

Or had she stayed and rocked the cuddly dog in the rocking chair for the whole hour, she would have learned something different but every bit as vital. This is the kind of learning that affects personality, that becomes part of a child's behavior. By comparison, the story of " Jesus, the Children's Friend," the song of church bells, the prayer would have been, for Carol, superficial. Instead, Carol discovered in Alice Todd an understanding friend. Is it not possible that out of that experience, the story of " Jesus, the Children's Friend," and the conversation and prayer about the doctors who are children's friends, had real meaning and personal significance for Carol because Carol had herself experienced this meaning?

FOR YOU TO THINK ABOUT

1. Select a three-year-old whom you know well and list his characteristics.

    a. Write down all you know about him.
       Write down what you do not know about him.

    b. What do you think is his most pressing developmental task?

2. What kind of a person does this three-year-old think he is? How does he feel about himself? That is, what self-image does he have? Collect evidence for this by noting remarks he makes, how he plays, what he chooses to play with, whom he chooses for friends, how he relates himself to you, his teacher.

CHAPTER TWO

Christian Growth Through Personal Relationships

Cᴀɴ ᴄʜɪʟᴅʀᴇɴ " learn " to be Christian? Surely, if the test of real learning is a change in attitude and behavior, they can. Without saying that nature has nothing to do with a person's becoming a mature Christian, we can assert without fear or equivocation that nurture has a great deal to do with it.[1] The Sunday church school movement is based on this assumption, as are fellowship groups, Christian prayer groups, and, in fact, the church itself. Children can grow up with Christian convictions and practices. The question we keep asking ourselves, our curriculum writers, and our Christian leaders, is: how? How do children grow into mature Christians? What are the steps in this process? How do we teach children to become Christian? If there is something more than songs, stories, projects, and activities, what is it? And how do we do it? These are not easy questions to answer, and yet we must answer them if we are not to fail in our task of Christian education.

The word that is the clue to the answer for each of these

---

[1] Even the sudden and dramatic conversion that has been the experience of many Christians through the years does not rule out nurture. Nurture-conversion is not an either-or way to mature Christian living. They go along together. Does not each new insight into God's will for one's life involve a conversion?

questions is "relationship." It is in a relationship of love and trust, respect and forgiveness that a child learns to love and trust, respect and forgive. Being treated as a person by men and women, parents and teachers who are themselves mature Christian persons is the fundamental experience for growth into Christian maturity. In this relationship of person to person the values, the integrity, the faith, the struggles, the joys of each person are treated with respect and understanding by the other person. Each person finds himself less defensive and fearful and more able to extend himself in an expression of concern to the other.

The word "person" as it is used here in the phrase, "to treat a child as a person," has more than the common-sense meaning of treating him as a member of the human race. Rather it is to think of him as a being of infinite worth. He is not only the child of Harry and Jane Brown; he is also a child of God — winsome, unique, creative — who expresses the nature of his Creator in his laughing, his loving, his forgiving, his boundless energy, his rejection of façade and insincerity. A person is an end in himself. He is not to be used to serve any other end.

Therefore, to treat a child as a person is to live with him as though he were an honored guest for whose life we are responsible. It is to be concerned about his needs, considerate of his moods, respectful of his person and of his possessions. Contrariwise, it is not to use him, manipulate him, or dominate him. There are too many parents and teachers in the world who use children to enhance their own feelings of worth or prestige; or to provide a channel for their own frustrated ambitions; or as an outlet for their own unexpressed hurts; or, by enforcing strict discipline and rigid behavior patterns, to give themselves a sense of power and influential position. A child, in this kind of relationship, becomes an object, a tool in the hands of another, a means to another's end, an "it." For an adult to commit such a sin against a child "it would be better for him if a great millstone were hung round his neck and he were thrown into the sea." A person is a "Thou," a child of God.

The parent or teacher who would treat a child as a person, a

" Thou " rather than an " it," must also maintain his own sense of personhood as a member of God's creation. He, too, is a son of God and, therefore, must not be used or thought of as an " it " whose sole function is unflagging service to the child's every whim. The parent or teacher is an " I." Therefore, the relationship of one person to another person is an " I-Thou " relationship; not " I-it," nor " it-Thou," nor, worse, " it-it."

Admittedly, children are likely to be unskilled in this kind of living. But many adults are, too. A child learns to live this way by being valued and regarded as this kind of person. The trouble with us adults who cannot treat children in this fashion is that we, in our growing up, were not treated as persons, and we are still trying to establish our sense of worth and value and prestige in our own eyes by using people to help us do it, especially the children about us, for they are the most vulnerable. There is considerable truth in the observation that most of us tend to treat children pretty much as we were treated by adults when we were children.

This " I-Thou," or person-to-person, relationship with children does not produce rude, undisciplined, self-centered children, *if the adults in the relationship insist on maintaining their personhood.* For example: John's mother respects his right to have, augment, or dispose of his collection of grubby sticks and uninteresting stones; and John must in turn respect his mother's buttons, bows, and various odd things that are available in every single drawer of the old sewing machine. The teacher does not interrupt John when he is talking or make a request of him when he is deeply engaged in something, nor does John interrupt her.

Adults do not take things from children without asking, nor do children take things from adults or from other children without asking. Adults do not tease children, or fool them, or misinform them, nor do children tease each other or " lie " to adults. The same kind of respect, consideration, and thoughtfulness which adults must accord children if adults would treat them as persons, adults must also expect for themselves. If they do not, the child grows into a boorish, unfeeling adult with no concern for the feelings or rights of others. If, on the other hand, adults demand "respect" of children without granting it, and courtesy without extending it, the child either grows into Mr. Milquetoast, the prey of any authoritarian person or idea that accosts him, or he becomes an adult who fights authoritarianism on every hand, dominates all whom he can (wife and children, the neighbors, public servants, and so forth), and has a hard time living with superiors or bosses whom he cannot dominate. To state the matter succinctly: children grow into real persons, whole persons, by being treated as real persons by adults who are themselves real persons, whole persons. Children grow into mature Christian persons through an "I-Thou" or *personal relationship* with mature Christian persons.

The Mature Christian Person

Let us now look at the mature Christian. What is he like, how do we recognize him?

There are three significant roots to the thoughts and actions of the Christian: how he feels about himself; how he feels about others; and how he feels about the world around him. This does not mean just vague, indefinable "feelings," but what *ideas* and *attitudes* he holds toward these three things.

First, the Christian thinks of himself as an adequate person, capable, with God's help, of handling whatever the day holds. He is confident that he is worth something to the life about him. His energies flow out in the service of long-term goals and purposes: justice, mercy, brotherhood. He believes in the ultimate triumph of goodness, and neither personal misfortune nor world-wide disaster of H-bomb proportions can destroy this faith. He is an active member of the world of men, purposing, deciding, choosing, working, serving them and God. Conversely, he is not withdrawn, walled-in, fearful, or anxious.

Second, the Christian thinks of other people as individual persons like himself with the same needs, the same hopes, the same sorrows and frustrations as he experiences. All men are made in the image of God, are God's children, and he, the Christian, is brother to all. The Christian feels himself responsible to and for these brothers, the ones he knows intimately as well as the ones in some Arab refugee camp or Indian village that he will never see. The Christian belongs to human society and is inextricably part of it.

Because the mature Christian is a real person in the psychological sense of that word, his evaluation of himself as adequate, competent, worth while, and acceptable is precious to him and he seeks in every situation to behave in such a manner as to preserve and maintain these ideas about himself. At the same time, he tries by his words and actions to create for the people about him the chance to be or to become persons, too. He treats everyone he meets in such a way that the other person feels adequate, able to handle his own life, worth while, and acceptable to people. Being a person himself, he treats others as persons.

Third, the Christian's attitude toward the world of nature is one of awe, wonder, great enjoyment, and great appreciation. The Creator has placed him in the midst of a universe so vast, so amazing, so bountiful that everything he learns about it leaves him more awed and more deeply humble. The Christian walks with gladness through the world, using it and at the same time preserving it for the use of others, enjoying its life and beauty and seeking to produce more life and beauty for others to enjoy. Likewise, with the world of things — money, possessions, wealth — the Christian considers himself God's steward in these matters, and he seeks constantly to use these gifts as God would want them used, in his name and to his glory.

The Christian is a person different from other men, and this difference lies at the very core of his living. It cannot be seen from the outside, so at first blush the Christian looks like anyone else. Other men often emulate his behavior, expounding the same reasons and ideas in the same words he uses, so that even a second look at him might lead us to think he is like many other men. But he isn't, and the difference lies deep within him. It is found in his relationship to God. He sees himself, his relationship to the world of men, and the rhythms and wonders of the universe all as part of God's creation. The Christian knows he does not understand all things, but he does not need answers to every " why " and " wherefore " in order to do God's will. His is a dedicated life that grows through prayer, meditation on the Scriptures, a maturing relationship to Jesus Christ, and fellowship within the church. He seeks to make of every experience an opportunity to be of greater service to God and man.

Yes, the Christian is different from the center of his being out, and it all springs from this interior model he carries in his mind's eye of himself, of the world of people, and of God. The Christian sees himself as a child of God. From this understanding of himself springs the behavior we call Christian: service to others without counting the cost to self; the generous giving of self, talents, and possessions to some cause or need; social action; active relationship to a church; the faithful practice of prayer, both with the worshiping congregation and by himself.

The problem for us who are teachers or parents — in fact, for anyone who has an active relationship with children — is now quite clear. When does this growth into mature Christian personhood begin? And how does God become the focal point for a person's life?

Christian Nurture Begins at Birth — The Growing Self

The point of the beginning is the growth and development of the Self; that consciousness each of us has of the kind of person we are, the kind of things we do well or poorly, our status and prestige in the eyes of our family and our community. All our behavior is a clue to the kind of Self — the kind of person — we think we are.

A Self can be ego-centered, withdrawn, fearful, anxious, filled with hate and hostility, scarred, hurt, misunderstood, mistreated. The world has too many Selves like that: the racists; the demagogues; the gossips; the " queers "; the violent-tempered; the juvenile delinquents; the emotionally and socially maladjusted

22

both within and without our mental hospitals, detention homes, and penitentiaries.

Or a Self can be loving, forgiving, trusting; extending its warmth, its concern to people on every hand; able to identify with (feel with) their hurts, rejoice with their joys, help with their burdens. This kind of Self is self-giving as contrasted with the other Self whose whole effort is self-protection. The self-protecting Self is engaged in a constant battle to assert its significance or save its integrity in the midst of what it considers a hostile world. The fearful, hostile Self is walled-in, defensive. The loving Self is outgoing, a part of all the life about it.

Many theologians today do not hold that a child is born with one kind of Self or the other. The possibility is present for each of us to become either kind of Self. The determining factors are the kinds of experiences we have since first we are warmed and fed and loved, or are denied warmth and food and love. Every experience, good and bad, makes some difference in forming this emerging self.

Psychologists know this, pediatricians recognize this, teachers hear about it in their teacher training courses, but too many of us know too little about it. If the infant's first needs are met — if he is fed when hungry, soothed and made comfortable when in distress, loved and held and cared for — his beginning impressions are that the world is a friendly and dependable place. He associates these pleasant experiences with his mother's face. As this first mother-child relationship continues, the child happily responds in trust to his father and brothers and sisters and any other member of the family unit. Finding himself acceptable, a person of worth, respected and loved in his family group, he enlarges his world step by step to include the children he plays with on the street, their parents, his first teacher, the mailman, the doctor, his " sitters," and anyone else with whom he makes personal contact.

If the child's experiences with each of these people are " person-producing " — that is, if the child finds himself acceptable to them, with significance and worth in their eyes — his emerging self is growing in the direction of the self of the mature Christian.

Let us illustrate this.

Mrs. Allen was watering the plants in the three-year-old room before she closed the door on another Sunday session. She noticed Sally standing quietly, watching.

" Sally, would you like to water the plants in our room? "

" I can't. That's a careful thing, and I can't do careful things."

" What happens, Sally? "

" Oh, I always spill the water, and Mother says that I make a big mess."

" I'll tell you what, Sally. You just fill the watering can and water the plants the best you can, and when you're finished you can wipe up the spills. I keep a sponge right here because sometimes I have a spill, too. It doesn't really matter how perfectly you do it. If the plants get a drink, and we wipe up the drops so the window sills won't be ruined, that's what matters."

Sally looked unbelievingly at Mrs. Allen, and then said, " I don't think I can do it."

" I think you can, Sally, and if you have trouble I'll be right here, putting away the crayons and books, and I'll help you." Sally took the watering can and spent ten minutes carefully tending to all the plants. She wiped up the drops with the sponge, and then almost shouted with delight, " I did it! I watcred them all by myself, and it was a careful thing, too."

Here Sally had a thrilling experience of feeling adequate. Her previous expcriences, probably growing from a too-tidy, too-perfectionist mother, had given her the conviction about herself that she could not do " careful things," that she was messy, that she caused work. She could have had quite a different picture of herself as competent, able to remedy accidents, and a help at home, if the very first plant-watering episode had been accompanied by a helping hand at the watering pot and a clean-up rag or sponge as part of the equipment.

Miss Don, toward the close of a happy Sunday morning, overheard Jimmy say to George, " You're a little boy." She glanced in Jimmy's direction and saw George, who really was small for his three years, standing close to the wall with Jimmy, Ricky, and Rosemary, all sturdy, tall children, in front of him. There seemed to be no hostility in their voices or postures. The three of them were merely making an observation, although they spoke somewhat accusingly.

George answered quickly, " No, I'm not a little boy, I'm a big boy."

" No, you're not," said Ricky, " you aren't as big as me."

" Or me," Jimmy added.

" In fact," said Rosemary, " I bet you're not big enough for this nursery group. You belong with the *little, little* kids."

Miss Don approached the group as George's chin began to quiver.

" You know, children, growing up is an interesting thing. Some people grow big, others not so big. It's just like the trees in front of our church — some are lots bigger than the others. And like dogs — some dogs grow big, others don't grow into big dogs.

" It doesn't really matter how big anyone is. What matters is how grown-up he acts. George is as grown-up as all the rest of us. He can do the things we do, he understands the stories we read, he's learning to take turns and to play with other children, just like all of us are. George belongs here all right even if he isn't very tall. He's grown-up on the inside and that's what matters."

What George needed to know was not just a statement of his height and weight. He was wondering, " Do I belong here? Do the others like me? Can I stay? " George needed to feel that he *belonged*, was acceptable to the group and to his teacher.

Such experiences as these — of being loved and respected, of building a sense of adequacy, of feeling worth while and acceptable to the people with whom you live — have been part of every child who is outgoing, friendly, eager for new experiences, willing to try the untried, able to approach strange adults and other children with confidence. This is the beginning of a child's trust in other people, thus opening one of the channels by which he comes to God.

God Becomes Part of the Child's World
Through Personal Relationships

Some of the children, having washed their hands and had their juice, joined their teacher for music around the piano.

She told the children that if they could sit very quietly for a minute they could hear something in their room that they hadn't noticed before.

" Listen, what do you hear? "

They were very quiet, and then several voices murmured, " Rain."

" What does it sound like? Can you make a little noise like the rain? " Christie pursed up her lips into a tight little hole and went " cheep, cheep, cheep." Someone else went " sh-h-h-h-h."

" Do you know that when Christie woke up this morning she looked out her window? What did she see? "

" Rain."

"And when Robert woke up this morning he heard a little noise, and he opened his eyes wide and sat up in bed and looked around, and what did he see? "

" Rain."

" Yes, rain on his windowpane. And when John and Sue and Carol woke up this morning what did they see and hear? "

" Rain."

" Boys and girls, when you saw and heard the rain this morning what did you think of? "

Kay said, " I thought of my new blue raincoat and hood and umbrella."

" Did you, Kay? That's the one your mother bought you in the East, isn't it? "

Fletcher said, " I thought of ' Rain, rain, go away; come again another day.' "

Kay said, " I thought I would like to get dressed and go out in it."

" I would, too, Kay," the teacher answered, " but I think most of the children don't have the right kind of clothes for rain today. Where does the rain come from? "

Fletcher said, " High in the sky."

" What is the rain good for? "

Robert said, " It makes the flowers grow."

" That's right, Robert; rain makes things grow."

" How do we get rain? " the leader asked.

Skippy said, " God makes it."

" Yes, Skippy. God planned for rain so that things could grow. You know those big dark clouds we see sometimes? They are rain clouds. When they get just so big and full of rain that they can't hold any more, they break up and all the rain comes down to the earth. It patters on the roof tops, splashes on the window-panes, dances in the street, and soaks into the ground, and everything gets a good cool drink — the trees and the grass and the flowers. . . ."

"And the bushes? "

" Yes, the bushes. Everything . . . and when this rain is over, the sun will shine warmly on the wet earth, and the wind will blow, and all the puddles will dry up, and we won't need to wear our rubbers outside. The rain goes back up into the air in tiny, tiny drops — so small we can't see them, and these drops go higher and higher up into the sky, and finally they gather together and make another big rain cloud. The cloud gets bigger and bigger until it falls apart and all the rain comes back down to the earth.

" That's how God planned for rain to come. It's a pretty good system, don't you think? "

A few nodded an assent. Most of them seemed to be lost in thought. The leader was beginning to wonder if this attempt at a simple explanation of quite a complex phenomenon was more confusing than awe-inspiring. Then she saw Christie with her forefinger extended, lowering her hand to the floor and then raising it above her head. Her arm relaxed, and by the third time she did it, her whole body responded to the movement.

" I know," Christie said excitedly, " it's like a bouncing ball. It

27

comes down (she quickly got to her feet and then squatted) and goes up (she stretched as high as she could on her tiptoes), comes down and goes up, comes down and goes up."

"That's just the way it does, Christie." The teacher was as joyous about the discovery as Christie was. "Would you all like to play raindrops while I play some rain music on the piano?"

Not all liked to, but several did. The rest watched and then the group sang "Rain Is Falling Down." In the quiet five seconds that followed the song the teacher bowed her head and said, "Dear God, we are glad for the rain that washes the world clean and makes the plants grow. Amen."

This experience of a teacher with a group of children learning about rain conveys some of the wonder and delight children experience when they discover new things about a rather commonplace event. It was fun for the children to talk about the rain and to think about the rain and to feel the teacher's appreciation for the rain. There was a brief solemn moment, when the mystery of the out-of-doors, and the quiet assurance that God was in charge of it all, added new dimensions to each child's notion of what the world is like and how he fits into it. The experiences of planting seeds, raking or gathering leaves, watching a bird build a nest, seeing a moth emerge from a cocoon, feeling an icicle melt, hearing the wind blow through the trees — all of these and more — can become part of the child's picture of a dependable world in the care of a great and loving God, if the adult sharing the experience with the child has such a conviction about God and conveys it to the child.

Just as a child learns of life and death and growth from a teacher or parent who sees these as part of God's creation, so he learns that the patterns of love and trust, and treating all people as persons created in the image of God, are also part of God's plan. They are, in fact, one of the ways through which God is at work in the world of men. These are not interpretations a nursery child can readily understand, but they are experiences out of which such interpretations, when they do come, acquire dramatic and convincing meaning.

What Kind of Person Must a Nursery Teacher Be?

It is clear that the teacher who would help a child grow into a mature Christian must be more than an earnest lay person who knows how to keep order and use the curriculum material, or a kindly someone who " doesn't know much about it but just loves little children."

The most important criterion for selecting a nursery leader is that she be a mature Christian herself (or himself), dedicated to making the gospel of love real in her own life as well as in the lives of others.

The nursery teacher must be a person, so that she will be sensitive to the child's efforts to find his Self and free enough to respond to *his need* rather than feeling attacked, frustrated, or inadequate as a result of his actions or words. When Mitchell says to her with great vehemence and hostility, " I don't like you and I'm going to chop this old church down," her first thought will be, " Mitchell's angry. Something has hurt him or seemed unfair or frustrated him. I must help him."

It is easy to think, " What a bad thing Mitchell said! Of course, he doesn't mean it. I'll josh him out of it." Or, " You don't know it, but I don't like you much either, Mitchell. You make me uneasy. If a mother happened in and heard you say that, what would she think I've been doing to you? What will the other children think? I must rebuke you." Neither the teacher who is shocked nor the one who feels attacked will be an adequate teacher for Mitchell.

No emotional crisis, no explosion of deep feelings, no infantile regressions, no unacceptable behavior should confuse and upset the nursery teacher. She should have such an understanding of three-year-olds that she knows almost what to expect, and she should be secure enough in her own right that the unexpected does not destroy her feeling of adequacy as a teacher.

Probably none of us is able to keep up such a high level of performance all the time. Teachers have good days and " off " days, just as the children do. However, the mark of the good teacher, the growing teacher, is that she studies the experiences which she feels she handled poorly and learns from them. She grows through her puzzlements, her mistakes.

The nursery teacher as a Christian person will have a genuine delight in and concern for the growth of each child. She thinks of each child as a person engaged in a great struggle to find himself, and of herself as the person standing at his side to help however and whenever he needs it, as much as he needs it. She covets for him a life in which he is able to handle his fears, anxieties, misapprehensions, experiences of distrust. She knows he cannot love a world he fears, or work for the salvation of men from narrow, cheerless lives if, in his own life, he has known failure and unacceptance at the hands of people.

This kind of teaching-learning-growing is exciting. It is individual for each child, growing out of his need in the direction he indicates. It is creative teaching, limitless in its possibilities. To do the job well requires faithful every-Sunday attendance on the part of the teacher, plus establishing a relationship with each child's home for at least the duration of the church school year. The experience for both child and teacher would have even greater depth and quality if one corps of teachers had the same group of children for two consecutive years.

Many churches are discovering that couples working together as teachers can do an excellent job in the preschool and primary grades. Some others have found that men make excellent nursery department teachers. This is as it should be. The essential qualifications for this job do not depend upon one's sex. To come to know well a man " in my church " with whom the children can be friendly and upon whom they can depend is an experience we should covet for our children. For some of our children such a man would be much different from their fathers; for others he would support and enhance their fathers. Whatever the case, the experience with some " daddy " other than the child's own, who is the kind of person here described, is so valuable both for the children and for the church that it is worth every effort to recruit and train the right men.

The Heart of the Program

What goes on in the church school on Sunday mornings grows directly out of this point of view that *what happens to the child is more important than the words, the equipment, the rituals, the symbolism that surround him.*

The physical environment is important. The room should be equipped with the play equipment suitable for three-year-olds: a housekeeping corner with table, chairs, dishes, dolls with clothes, beds, doll carriage; a block corner with large building blocks that are unit-dimensional and with cars and trucks; a table and a few chairs for the creative art materials center — paste, paper, clay, crayons, paint; a quiet corner where the books and puzzles are. (For more information about the room, see chapter three.)

This is an environment that reaches out with a beckoning finger and says, " Come, play with me. Try me out. Experiment here. Come, at your own speed, with your own skills, and do what you will in the direction you need to go today."

The teacher has the same idea that the room suggests. " Here we have provided for you, the children. Bring here your problems, your excitements, your hurts, your hopes, and we'll work at them together. I'll help with a light touch and a prayer for wisdom."

This she does. She watches David create an Easter bunny and a basket of eggs out of clay. As he tells her about it, he picks up the basket of eggs, knocks the bunny flat with them, and quickly and vigorously pounds the whole business into a gray mass.

" Well, you did away with that fellow, didn't you? " she remarks.

" Yes, I did," he answers vehemently, " and I hope he never comes back again."

Having expelled that bad feeling, David spends ten minutes feeding, dressing, and wheeling the baby in the doll carriage. Then he joins the block play, but he runs his cars so vigorously on the superhighway that he knocks it apart. Donald objects and David leaves, giving the car a terrific kick into the wall.

He spends a few minutes in the rocking chair, seeing and hearing nothing in the room, apparently lost in daydreams.

"Something's wrong with David. He's confused, hurt, angry. Oh, that I might help," the teacher thinks, looking at the books on the children's table, not wanting to intrude on David's world, yet wanting achingly to provide a way for him to talk about it. Her eyes light on "In My House," a book brought from home.

She invites him to hear the story. He listens intently, quietly, disclosing not a thing but appearing to relax. The hour ends.

David's grandmother accompanies his mother as she stops for David. The teacher hears grandmother ask, "What goes on in this room, Mary?"

"I've never attended the full hour," David's mother replies, "but they seem to have a wonderful time *playing* here. David can't wait until Sunday comes. It's funny, too, because he has lots of the same toys at home, some even better. . . ."

Contrary to widespread notion, the three-year-old program of the church school need not be "just play" on the one hand or rote learning of Bible verses, meaningless prayers, or poor, ditty-like music on the other. A child grows into a mature Christian person neither by fortuitous chance nor by being imbued with words and ideas — however excellent they are and however skillfully they are "taught." Some Christian education programs let the children grow "like Topsy," seeking to provide for them a "happy time in church" with gentle, kindly teachers who really like children. Other programs are based on sound curriculum materials that deal with the facts of our faith, the stories, traditions, and practices of Christianity, and teachers are "trained" to use this material properly so that children will "learn" it.

There is some merit in both these methods. But even combining the methods provides no really clear way to aid a child in the process of growing toward Christian maturity. The leader needs to understand how personality develops, and how people grow in love and trust and self-giving, and then she can work on "How to Teach" with intelligence.

There are sound reasons why any church should invest the

nursery program with the best leadership and facilities it can provide. The nursery program has the same goal as has every other program of the church school: namely, to help a child grow into a mature Christian person. The method of the nursery program — establishing a personal " I-Thou " relationship with each child — requires skilled Christian teachers. Its tools are an environment of *things* that offers each child many opportunities for growth in creative expression, skill, and sense of adequacy, and of *persons* that become for each child a channel of God's love and truth, understanding and forgiveness.

To set up such a program requires much dedicated effort on the part of the teachers and the church leadership. But to stop short of doing the best we know how to do is to shirk our obligation to children and to deny our responsibility as Christian teachers.

FOR YOU TO THINK ABOUT

1. a. Stephanie has attended the three-year-old group for three Sundays. It looks as though she will stand for another entire morning holding the cuddly kitten and watching. What may Stephanie be " saying to you " ? How can you, her teacher, treat her as a person?

   b. Terry comes " busting " into the room, knocks down blocks, steps on a puzzle on the floor, sweeps the crayons from the table, and heads for the housekeeping corner. What may he be telling you about himself? How can you treat him as a person?

   c. How is treating a child as a person different from indulging him, spoiling him?

2. How does a continuing relationship with mature Christian persons help a child become a mature Christian?

3. What did the teacher do that made the church school experience helpful for David? (See episode on page 31.)

4. How have experiences of knowing Christian persons helped you in your own Christian life and growth?

CHAPTER THREE

The Sunday Program for Three-Year-Olds

T HE CHURCH that really intends a program of Christian education for the three-year-old will secure the very best physical environment and leadership the church can provide. The teaching personnel, space, and equipment all are important. In chapters two, three, four, ten, and eleven there is material on the qualifications of the teacher for nursery age children. Let us now turn to a description of the room and equipment required for the program for three-year-olds.

The Environment Teaches

The room needs to be light, cheerful, clean, warm on the floors, with windows low enough for children to look out of, and located, preferably, on the first floor of the building. There should be 30 to 35 square feet of floor space for each child, one teacher to each six children, never fewer than two teachers with a group of children. Bathroom facilities should be close at hand.

In a quiet corner, there should be a rug where the children can look at books, work puzzles, listen to stories, sing songs. If a piano is available it should be next to the rug. A low table on which is placed the offering basket, a Bible, and other articles such as a picture and flowers should also be at the edge of the rug. (Candles are not used on the table for they signify a symbolism not understandable to the young child.) The only chair on the rug should be a low one for the teacher to use when she tells a story or sings with the children. If she does not need the chair, all the better. The children sit on the rug, facing the teacher, and cross their legs tailor fashion, so their feet do not get in other children's way.

In another place in the room there should be a work table about 18 inches high. This will be used by the children for crayon work, clay, painting, cutting and pasting, and for other activities such as planting seeds in the spring, or a bulb to bloom for Easter, or making Christmas presents. This table should not be far from the door leading to the bathroom, so that paste and clay can be washed away without too much hazard to walls and to other children passed en route. A large bulletin board area near this table, hung at the eye level of the children, will prove useful for picture and other displays. 952679

There should be a housekeeping corner with several dolls of various types such as a baby doll, a girl and a boy doll, dolls representing various racial groups, all having clothes with buttons or snaps of a medium size so the clothes can be taken off and put on by the children. A doll bed, a doll carriage, doll high chair, tea table and chairs (child size), and dishes of good plastic material or of metal with no sharp edges should also be in the housekeeping corner. A cupboard, stove, ironing board, iron, and a chest of drawers with " dress up clothes " for the children are desirable.

Blocks and trucks occupy another corner of the room. Here roads, garages, airports, houses, lumberyards, and churches are built Sunday after Sunday. The blocks should be smooth, unit-dimensional: that is, the larger ones are exactly two, four, or eight times the size of the smallest block. Preferably, the blocks should be unpainted. Ordinary toy and department stores rarely carry this type of block. The blocks can be made by someone in the church or community or purchased from nursery school equipment and supply houses. A variety of cars and trucks should be near the blocks. Three-dimensional figures of people and of animals greatly contribute to the children's play in this corner.

Avoid spending money on cheaply constructed, sharp-edged,

pressed-steel cars, trucks, trains, and airplanes. They are a disappointment, for they bend or break (as do most plastic toys) or lose their wheels. Usually wind-up and friction toys also are not good choices. Choose instead sturdy cast-steel or wooden trucks, some that haul, some that tow, some that can be sat upon and ridden. A few other pieces of equipment such as a pounding board, one or two rather complicated block stacks, a wooden shoe to be laced, perhaps a few washable cuddly toys will provide individual activity for a child who needs and wants to be working on something all by himself.

All the toys and all the blocks should be arranged on open, low shelves available to the children. So should sheets of paper about 12 x 18 inches in size, large crayons, paste, and clay. Books should be on the book table.

An easel equipped with three jars of tempera paint (red, yellow, and blue), a long-handled paint brush for each jar, and a plastic apron or man's shirt made into a coverall will provide another activity enjoyed by three-year-olds.

Nursery departments of churches are often given used toys and equipment by church families whose children have outgrown them. Sometimes these are good toys for the nursery room; often they are not. They may be " gadgets," or suitable only for older children (such as a doll's house), or duplications of equipment already in the room, or in poor condition. It is probably wisest to accept all such gifts with the understanding that if they are not needed they will be given to some other group — a settlement house, the Salvation Army, Boy Scout repair committee, or similar organization.

If the three-year-old program runs from one and a half to two hours, it is important to include a light snack of juice and crackers, and a quiet time when the children rest on small individual rugs or bath mats. The mats may be provided by the parents. This relaxing-resting period provides a " pick-up " for the children that helps them avoid the tiredness and the frictions that come from continued activity and the stimulation of being with other children. If the nursery program is held during the eleven o'clock worship hour, pausing for juice and crackers is still a good idea; but lying down to rest is not necessary.

A Look at the Program

Recalling some of the experiences of Alice Todd on Sunday morning (see chapter one) will give us a pretty clear picture of how a morning program runs. At the beginning of the church school year there is no total group activity as such for three-year-olds. Most activities run along at the same time, engaged in by two or three or even four children who may or may not be playing together. Most likely the children will be playing beside each other. The teachers may decide that the total group will go for a walk, or plant crocuses in the churchyard. But if the children have a choice, very likely there will be some who will prefer to play with clay or work puzzles. Later, when the children are four, or approaching this age, the total group may voluntarily gather on the rug for a story and song and conversation time, and the children will be able to participate in the experience together for five or seven minutes before they become too restless. But this is not likely to occur in the fall and winter when the children are younger and still adjusting to one another, to their new adult friend, and to an environment that offers unlimited possibilities for creative and imaginative play.

The exact order of the morning's activities will change from time to time as the children become acquainted with their nursery room and as they grow older. Generally speaking, it suits the child best to have the room set up when the hour begins and, therefore, this is the best way for teacher and child to become acquainted. Each child chooses what he wants to do as he enters the room, and he is free to move from one activity to another all during the free play period which probably should last for forty-five to fifty minutes of the hour. Going to the bathroom and getting a drink can be done by each child as he feels the need to do these things. Toward the end of the hour, the teachers can help the children draw their activities to a close and put away the toys until next Sunday.

One teacher should be sitting at the edge of the rug reading stories, telling stories, singing, or doing finger plays so that, as the children finish what they are doing, they can join the group on the rug and look at books themselves or participate with the others in whatever activity is taking place. This may be the time when a prayer follows a particularly good story. It will not always be. The real prayer of the morning may have been said when some of the children held a little brown crocus bulb and looked at a picture of the flower which the teacher told them their bulb would grow to be. The prayer may be voiced by a child as he relates a particularly significant event in his life, and then it is his prayer. Some Sundays there may not be a spoken prayer, but it would be quite clear to the wise observer that the quality of the living that went on in the room was both prayer and praise.

The teachers work together in the nursery group according to a previously agreed-upon plan. Each one knows which part of the room she will have as her " station ": who will greet the children; who will supervise the bathroom; who will conduct the quiet activity on the rug, and so forth. The teachers may take turns by Sundays with these responsibilities, or they may decide to stay with one sphere of activity for some time. It does not matter how this is arranged so long as each teacher is having an opportunity to share in the planning and the execution of the program.

The nursery home visitor — if she is not also a teacher — should be present on most Sunday mornings to greet the families as they arrive and to keep her relationship with them alive. If she can also visit the three-year-old group frequently enough to get to know the children and for them to know her, she will find home visiting more rewarding both to the family and to herself.

Who Administers the Nursery Department Program?

Various people may administer this program, depending on the size and number of groups which the church provides in its nursery department. If the nursery department consists solely of a group for three-year-olds, one of the teachers of that group usually assumes the responsibility for the administrative details of keeping records, ordering supplies, arranging for housekeeping details, and calling teachers' meetings. However, if the nursery department consists of two or more groups, it is probably more satisfactory, for everyone, to have a superintendent of the department who is appointed by the board or committee of Christian education and who is not also a teacher. It is his or her task to see to it that the rooms have been cleaned and are warm each Sunday, that each room has a complete teaching staff, that announcements and notices get to the right places and right people on time, that supplies are on hand and easily available to the teachers, that the necessary records are kept. Depending on how the rest of the church school is supervised, it might be the task of the superintendent to set up and plan the teacher training sessions that run throughout the year. He or she also is probably responsible for recruiting new teachers.

The superintendent, along with the nursery visitor, welcomes new families who come into the church, tells them of the program and facilities available for nursery children, and introduces the families to the teacher of the age group in which their children will be enrolled.

The nursery department, like the other departments of the church school, is under the leadership of the board or committee of Christian education of the church. This is the board responsible for the philosophy of Christian education which the church follows and for the curriculum materials which it uses. The total church school program, parent and adult education, and the youth groups are all administered by this board. The nursery department should have a direct relationship to this board, either through its superintendent who is a member, or through another person who represents the total church school on the board. It is the responsibility of this board, among other things, to decide for which age groups the church will provide, how the available space in the church building can best be used, what policies regarding registration and church-home relationships will exist. For example, many churches require a preregistration of all children whose parents intend to bring them to the three-year-old or a younger group. This makes it possible for the teacher to visit the homes of the children before the children come to the church and for the teacher and the three-year-old to become acquainted. It also gives the visitor a chance to describe to the parents the church's program for young children, and for the parents to ask questions about their part in the program.

The Three-Year-Old Program During the Morning Worship Period

It has been implied that everything that happens to a child in the church becomes for him an experience for good or ill, helping him grow in self-confidence and adequacy or leaving him scared, anxious, or insecure. It sometimes happens that a church has an excellent nursery program during the regular church school hour, but provides a haphazard, ill-planned sitting service for those children who come during the hour of morning worship. These children, too, are coming to their church; and they need and deserve an experience in their church that is up to the standard of the best the church can provide in leadership, program, and physical environment. The teachers must be as loving, as wise, and as faithful as are the other teachers in the nursery department. The program needs to be as carefully planned and as skillfully conducted as the program for the church school hour. And the equipment and the room should be of the type that invite the children to learn and to feel at home in their church. All that has been said about the program for the church school period is valid for *all other* programs provided by the church for its three-year-old children.

Three-Year-Olds and Special Days

There has been much thought given to the part nursery children should play in such all-church events as the family Thanksgiving service, the Christmas pageant, the Children's Day program and other celebrations. Too often the total church observance of events such as these brings nothing but bewildering confusion for the three-year-old. Frequently, it happens that he is either an onlooker being " shushed," or he is a performer in something meaningless to him, although sentimentally satisfying to the adult. With a little thought it becomes immediately clear how such experiences violate what we intend for three-year-olds. We want the church experience to be personally meaningful and creative for each child. All-church events usually do not lead to this result.

This does not mean, however, that the events of the church calendar can have no meaning for the three-year-old. The experience of being glad for good things (Thanksgiving), of feeling loved and cared for by listening to a story of how Mary and Joseph cared for their new baby (Christmas), of experiencing the meaning of love in his own relationships, an experience that gives meaning to the love Jesus had for people (Easter), or of wondering how little dead-looking seeds grow into green plants, and of being glad for the return of the flowers and birds and the warm weather (Easter and spring) — all these are meaningful to the three-year-old and should properly be included in the Sunday program for him. He will gain far more from having these experiences in his own group then he will from participating in a program that must necessarily be planned with the interests of older persons in mind. The all-church program is better saved until the child is older and able to participate in it with understanding and appreciation for what it has to offer.

One satisfying way to include three-year-olds in the Children's Day program is to plan a church school open house when each department of the church school invites parents to visit. During the year each group saves the completed project activity which the classes have worked out as part of their curriculum. The Saturday before Children's Day, the teachers and the children in the older departments set up their rooms (or their exhibit space in the church hall) with whatever materials they have that tell something of what has been done during the past year. Teachers in the three-year-old group can display their equipment and prepare pictures and posters that tell about the work of their program.

On Children's Day, either at the church school hour or in the late afternoon, parents and children go from room to room seeing what is on display, talking with the teachers, greeting their friends and neighbors. Each older child is host to his parents, telling them what his class has done and conducting them to the other rooms or exhibits. The three-year-olds do not leave their room but remain with their parents to enjoy together activities familiar to them from their Sunday morning experiences.

The event closes when the children conduct their parents to the sanctuary for a brief worship service using the order of worship and the hymns that the children know. The worship may be led by one or two teachers or the superintendent — whoever usually leads the worship for the grades of the church school. The minister of the church may have a part in the worship, but he probably will not conduct it, for he and the children are not used to working together, and this is the *Children's* Day. Three-year-old children, if they attend the closing worship with their parents, will admittedly be spectators more than participants. However, if the worship is no longer than ten minutes, the experience of being in the " big church," hearing the church music, and seeing their minister in front wearing his robe, if he wears one, can be significant even for three-year-olds.

Such a program as this has meaning for children and avoids the feelings of competition and rivalry, of inadequacy or loss of prestige, or of pride that inevitably follows the piece-speaking, song-singing Children's Day performance before the whole congregation.

Vacation Church School and the Three-Year-Old

Should three-year-olds be included in a vacation church school program? *Only* if the church can meet the needs of children this young. The vacation church school program usually runs as long each day as a nursery school program. It seems obvious, therefore, that the church which plans a vacation church school group for three-year-olds would do well to follow good nursery school standards and procedures in matters of space, equipment, trained leadership, and morning program. Chapter twelve on the weekday nursery school discusses these standards at greater length. However, it would not be amiss here to emphasize that:

1. Three-year-olds in a two-hour session *need* to lie down to rest for ten to fifteen minutes, and they need mid-morning juice and crackers. The rest period requires space with a cot or a rug for each child.

2. There should be not more than fifteen children to a room.

3. There must be a carefully planned introduction of the child to this new experience. Some children require two weeks to adjust to a daily group experience away from their mothers, and many schools last only this length of time.

The Minister and the Three-Year-Old

It is important for the minister to have a part in this church-home program of the nursery department. The children of the three-year-old group should come to know him as *their* minister, just as they come to identify the church as *their* church. And the parents of these children, especially those parents who are new in the fellowship of the church, need opportunities to meet and to know the minister. How this will take place depends upon the organization of each church and church school and upon the minister's own interest and skills.

Where the timing of the Sunday morning activities in the church makes it possible, frequent, unhurried visits to the three-year-old group by the minister will afford great satisfaction both to him and to the children. He may quietly join them at play in one part of the room, or engage a few children in conversation, or read a story to others.

Parents can learn to know him as their minister through their experience in Sunday morning worship. However, it is desirable if the minister can also participate in some of the parents' meetings, for there both minister and parents can really come to know each other.

It goes without saying that if a church-home program of Christian nurture is to be worth the effort, the minister must not only come to know the families of the church, but he must also strengthen, support, and counsel the lay people of the church school, the teachers, superintendents, home visitors, members of the board of Christian education, and others who are attempting to make the program effective.

FOR YOU TO THINK ABOUT

1. What is meant by the statement " the environment teaches "? What specific " teaching " goes on in the housekeeping corner, the block corner, at the work table, on the rug with books and puzzles and music?

2. Make a floor plan arrangement of your three-year-old room and sketch the activity materials and furnishings into the plan in the best possible fashion. How many children do you have room for? How many teachers should you have?

3. Take another look at the space and facilities available in your church for your three-year-old program. If your church is not able to meet the standards described in this chapter, what changes can you make now to improve your program? What changes can you make within the next month, the next year? Set up a plan for making these improvements.

4. How is the piece-speaking, song-singing program " put on " by the children of the church school before the whole congregation a violation of the child as a person, a " Thou " ?

PART TWO

Helping Teachers Learn to Teach

". . . I chose you and appointed you that you should go and bear fruit and that your fruit should abide; so that whatever you ask the Father in my name, he may give it to you. This I command you, to love one another."

John 15: 16, 17

CHAPTER FOUR

Teachers' Meetings to Help Teachers Grow

How does a mother, or any earnest and committed lay person, become a good teacher of young children? There are many who want to do a good job, who are faithfully trying to do a good job, but who do not know how well they are doing, and often there seems to be no way really to find out. The more a person teaches, the more relaxed she becomes as a teacher, the easier it is, and the more fun, too; but now and then she wonders if she is not simply growing more comfortable with the little phrases, techniques, and patterns she has developed, which may not have been the best ones in the first place.

The teacher who successfully establishes a personal " I-Thou " relationship with her children does not do so with one splendid stroke of skill and understanding. Quite the contrary. Such a relationship is a growing one. It begins in a small way, almost insignificantly. The growth is slow and not always a steady progress forward. For this reason, if the relationship is to have any depth, if the lives of teacher and children are to become engaged in mutual trust and understanding, faithful, every-Sunday attendance is necessary for both teacher and children. (Every-Sunday attendance is not possible for nursery children for many obvious reasons. But when children are well, regular attendance is essential and should not be interrupted by the whims — or the sleepiness — of parents.) If the same teachers can live with the same children in the church school group for two consecutive years, growth through the relationship is even greater.

How does a teacher gain new skills? How does she get some insights into her attitude toward children and how she is treating them? Can a teacher learn to have " a light touch " ? Can she acquire a sense of timing both for a child and for the group? Can she learn to treat a child as a person; allow him to make his own decisions insofar as he is able; help him to " save face " when he has made an assertion or taken a stand he really would like to get out of; accept him, in words and actions he will understand, as an important, worth-while, needed member of the group; help him succeed in becoming a co-operative, contributing member of the group, which every child really wants to be, by interpreting good intentions behind unacceptable behavior, by helping him correct his mistakes, by speaking to him positively instead of in " don'ts " and negations?

These are the " little things " that open the doors between a teacher and a child, that convince the child that his teacher believes in him, cares for him, and is trying to understand the world from his point of view. These " little things " are the marks of a good teacher. Because she has these skills with and convictions about children, she lives with children easily, happily. She feels competent, successful, able to handle anything that arises or to find the necessary help should she need it. She is a person. Most teachers would like to become this kind of person. Most trainers of teachers everywhere, in schools and institutes and workshops, hope that the teachers they are working with will become this kind of person.

How do teachers learn? The same way children learn, the same way anybody learns . . . teachers learn by becoming involved in a situation in which they have something at stake. They have said something, done something, decided something. They have entered into the situation with their minds alive and their energies free-flowing and in some manner they have committed themselves to the situation. This is different from just hearing about how to teach, or reading about it, or passively watching

48

other people teach. Until the learner, whatever his age, is personally involved in the learning, little, if any, change takes place in the way he acts or what he thinks. He may acquire gimmicks and some superficial techniques for doing some things better, but his basic patterns and understandings, which determine how he thinks about himself and treats other people, will be little changed.

The kinds of methods and materials used at most teachers' meetings — presentations, movies, slides, lectures, book or pamphlet study, working out plans and details for keeping attendance records, planning church school programs and exhibits, and so on — have merit in helping teachers learn only if the teachers are personally involved in what is going on. Quite often this is not the case. The problems dealt with, the questions faced, the interpretations provided may not grow out of the experience of any teacher present. At best such meetings provide learning and growing for only a few unless the material serves as an open door through which each teacher sees a new interpretation for her particular puzzlement.

There are other methods than these. Let us consider some of them.

The Study of Anecdotal Records

Alice Todd made some records of one of her children in the three-year-old group, and she and her teachers spent a meeting in studying the records.

Anecdotal Records on Leslie

2nd Sun. Oct. Today I met Leslie, her first day here since I've been teaching, but she made herself right at home, throwing blocks out of the boxes, kicking the little cars across the room, ripping sheets, blankets, and covers off the doll beds and hurling them and the dolls to the floor. Then to the dishes, which she spilled from the cupboard, the stove, and the shelf in glorious clattery confusion.

After each of these disruptions, Harriet or I said some such thing as, "We don't throw the blocks around; we build things with the blocks," or "You've torn apart the bed for Betsy's baby, and she's feeling bad. I'll help you put it together, so Betsy can go on playing." None of our remarks met any response. Leslie just walked away, and in a few seconds she was creating disorder in another corner.

She seemed to be enjoying herself, for she had a little half-smile on her face. So far as I could tell, none of the objections raised by the trespassed-against children affected her. She seemed not even to hear them.

After Leslie threw the dishes to the floor, I picked up a few and set them on the table and asked her if she would like to have a party with me. She would. She sat down quickly in one of the chairs. Two other children were also sitting at the table, and they joined the "pretend party" while Ross, a boy in the group, cooked and served the food. Leslie seemed to enjoy this and stayed with it for all of five minutes.

Something, I don't remember what, made me think she was through with the party, and I suggested that we had paper and paste out and Sue would help her get started. She pasted the rest of the hour, the longest time Harriet or Sue said they had ever seen her sit still.

3rd Sun. Oct. When Leslie came in this morning she went right to the table, sat down, and pasted pictures as fast as Sue could cut them out. Leslie produced half a dozen compositions to take home. Sue reported that she made no choice among the pictures she pasted; any one would do any place on the paper.

When some of the children were singing and listening to a story Leslie bustled all around the room, into one thing, then another. One or another teacher kept returning with her to the rug, but Leslie left about as soon as she got there. She was not unduly noisy, nor was she really occupied with anything. Just went from one thing to the other.

Finally, she began playing the piano, which I asked her not to do.

When the mothers came Leslie grabbed half a dozen small books from the desk and raced down the hall with them — to her mother's classroom.

4th Sun. Oct. Leslie peremptorily left after five minutes this morning to get her money for the offering from her mother who teaches in another room on this floor. Sue went with her. Leslie had done this before and also, as before, she carried the money around for most of the morning before finally being enticed into putting it in the jar.

I heard a mother, who was staying to help her daughter feel secure, say, "Little Girl, you shouldn't do that." I looked up. Leslie had taken the lid off the jar and had all the money in her hands and pockets. She left the table, and Sue started after her saying, "Put the money back, Leslie; that isn't what we do with the money." Leslie gave Sue an impish grin and began to hustle away.

A chase was in the making, so I cut it off. "Would you like to put all the money back by yourself, Leslie? I'll put the lid on the jar, and you can drop it all through the slot." Leslie did, and I put the jar up.

2nd Sun. Nov. This morning Leslie asked for the clay. She played with it with great interest for ten to fifteen minutes, making pancakes and rolling worms. She tried repeatedly to use the trucks and dishes with the clay, but when the teacher objected, Leslie complied without complaint.

Leslie went to the bathroom to wash her hands and made a great mess with the water, getting it all over the washbowl and the floor. Twice I have found her holding her finger over the fountain and squirting the hall. When I pointed out that she was splashing the floor where people walked as well as the coats hanging beside the fountain, Leslie made no response, just grinned and permitted me to walk her away from the temptation.

3rd Sun. Nov. This morning Leslie and Shelley together built three high block towers. As soon as one fell the children began to build again. Both of them called for the teacher to look. I did, and stood by watching the tower get higher. When the first tower fell under Shelley's block, Leslie said nothing, and proceeded to begin the second. They both looked as though they were enjoying the activity.

1st Sun. Dec. A big girl, I should judge her to be six years old, appeared at our gate in the middle of our morning, and stood a while looking all over the room.

"What can I do for you?"

"Nothing."

She went into the bathroom, shut the door, and in another minute I heard the sounds of a minor flood. I opened the door, rebuked her for making such a mess (finger-under-faucet technique), and suggested she return to her class.

"Is Leslie behaving herself?"

"I'm sure she is. Now you better hustle off."

She left. In five minutes there she was at the gate again searching the room with her eyes. She spied Leslie and called to her. Leslie didn't reply. I did.

"What do you want?"

"I just wanted to see if Leslie is behaving."

"Are you her big sister?"

"Yes."

"Leslie always behaves here, and she doesn't need you to look after her. You're the one who isn't behaving at this point. Now run along with you and let us alone." I was annoyed.

She left and didn't return.

2nd Sun. Dec. Today we began making Christmas presents, candle holders out of red and green dough-clay. Leslie spent the entire play period with the dough-clay. Most of the children enjoyed it, but not for that long.

A number of children made large pictures by pasting scraps of colored paper and cloth onto manila paper. Leslie wasn't interested in that.

When her mother came she saw many of the children taking their pictures home. She turned to Leslie, "Where's your picture?"

"I didn't make one."

"What did you do? Fooled around all morning again, I suppose."

3rd Sun. Jan. Leslie arrived late today, which is not usual with her. Her mother also was late for her class, so she left quickly without a good-by or any other word. I helped Leslie get her hat and snowsuit off and told her I was glad she had come.

She first found the truck that has the wagon tied to the back of it. She filled the wagon with blocks and drove it around the room for some time. The next time I noticed her she was piling blocks in very high towers on the little wagon. Mitchell unintentionally knocked one over, and she went toward him, complaining. I stepped over to the scene and offered to help her rebuild the tower on a steadier base. (Found five pennies under the second block which she ran and put into the jar when I said that they were causing the trouble.) I explained that Mitchell had not meant to bump it.

Somewhat later I helped her do the new policeman puzzle. She stayed with it one time through and then left. This was the first puzzle I had seen her do.

She also played with clay this morning. I discovered her washing her hands in the fountain because the bathroom was occupied. We waited until it was empty. I adjusted the hot and cold water for her and got a sniff of perfume.

"My, you smell good, Leslie. Did someone give you a bottle of perfume?"

"No, it's my mom's. She put it on me this morning."

I told a story about a snowman this morning and for the first time this year, to my knowledge, Leslie appeared interested in the story, responding several times with a quiet laugh or a nod of her head.

The mothers were there before we had finished, and in the confusion of getting the right pictures, purses, and so forth to the right little people, I didn't watch Leslie.

Soon the big sister was saying to me, "Where's Leslie?"

"I don't know. I suppose she's gone to your mother's room as she usually does."

"She shouldn't have done that. Mother's not there." And she was off.

A few minutes later Leslie, her mother, and big sister were back in the room. Leslie's mother was dressing her rather roughly, I thought, and both the mother and the big sister were scolding Leslie.

Discussing the Records

The teachers of the three-year-old group, Jane, Ellen, Harriet, and Alice Todd, spent the evening discussing these records, trying to understand what was happening to Leslie. Parts of a transcribed tape recording of their discussion follow:

Jane: This is very interesting. I didn't know anyone knew this much about Leslie . . .

Ellen: I witnessed some of these episodes, but they didn't have much meaning. Now that I see them in sequence with some others, they seem to be important — I mean they show something about Leslie that I hadn't thought of.

Alice: Like what?

53

Ellen: Well . . . like this last one. I saw her working on that puzzle with you; and it's right — she *did* listen through the *whole* story, but I hadn't remembered that this was the first time this year for either of those things. How do you account for it? Was she just feeling good?

Harriet: I wish I could have seen it. She certainly never did either of those things last year. She's changed tremendously.

Alice: I think she *has* changed somewhat, Harriet. She seems more relaxed, under less tension than when I first saw her in October.

Jane: How did it happen? What did we — or the rest of you — do? I admit that she's baffled me, and annoyed me, so I've left her to someone else.

Alice: One thing is that I think she's found acceptance here. She hasn't been bossed by a big sister or nagged at, harangued, suggested to, cautioned, admonished, at every hand. We've tried to make her feel that she's acceptable to us — in spite of her behavior — and that she's not bad.

Ellen: Judging from the way her mother treats her and the things she says to her even in front of us, I'll bet she's told she's a bad girl, always doing something wrong every day she lives. Don't you think so? Why . . . that day she spent the whole morning completely engrossed in making a candle holder for her mother — and then her mother scolded her for not having a picture to take home! I felt so bad for Leslie. You said something to her mother, didn't you, Harriet?

Harriet: Yes, I explained — it isn't on the record — that Leslie had done a fine job with our modeling material that morning and had spent a long time on it.

Alice: We're all pretty defensive for Leslie, or maybe I should say I am. I treated her big sister pretty brusquely, even unkindly, it appears to me now.

Jane: When?

Alice: That Sunday she kept checking up on Leslie . . . the first Sunday in December it was.

Harriet: I remember that episode. I was feeling the same way you were. Leslie was having such a good morning I didn't want her to be bothered. I kept wondering if Leslie's mother was sending the sister in to check up on her — and us.

Alice: So you were annoyed, too! That thought never occurred to me. I just didn't want the sister to interrupt Leslie, but it was a poor way to handle it. . . .

Jane: Something I've noticed is that you, Alice, often are able to turn something bad Leslie's doing — I don't mean bad, you know what I mean, like tearing the beds apart or knocking down the dish cupboard or someone's blocks — you seem to be able to get Leslie to put it back together and play with the stuff for a while — like you did in that first episode.

Harriet: I've noticed that, too. Every time I try to get her to put things back I get nowhere. She just walks off and in another minute is pulling something else apart.

Alice: Well, I'm not always successful either. But what we must try to do, I think, is to help Leslie channel or use this energy that's bursting out all over the place. She herself is really much happier doing something creative and constructive than tearing things apart. . . . It's almost as though something has to get out of her so fast that she can't control it herself. Just making her pick things up or put things back isn't helping this bottled up tension — I think that's what it is, really, not just coltish good spirits frisking its heels. So we have to help her relieve the tension by working it off, not bottle it up and add more to it by reprimanding her. You see, in that first episode Harriet and I both tried that, and it didn't work. Even the objections of the other children didn't faze Leslie, whereas some children would have been very much affected. I think what actually happened is not that Leslie picked up the dishes and put them back — I did most of that — but that we started to play tea party at almost top speed. I should have included those details in the record. Leslie ran and got a doll, put it in the high chair, fed it vigorously, put it back to bed, baked fish in the oven, served Betsy and me, sat down and jumped up half a dozen times to get something or take it away. Then she just seemed to have exhausted her ideas about the tea party, and I asked her if she wanted to paste. She did, and that saved the day — for her and us.

Ellen: I've noticed about that pasting, have the rest of you? She just loves to do it, and she uses huge gobs of paste and makes an awful mess on the paper and on her hands. None of the other children are so messy with it. . . . Why is that?

Alice: Pasting seems to be a very satisfying experience for Leslie, and Sue has helped Leslie as much as any of us by supplying her with an endless amount of pictures cut from magazines, paper, and dish after dish of paste. She never suggests how it should be done and never indicates that the finished product is something of a mess, and Leslie hardly misses a Sunday doing some pasting. She seems to love to squish it and pat it and mess around in it, doesn't she, Ellen? You supplied her needs a couple of Sundays when Sue wasn't there.

Ellen: That's right — and did you see her with that awfully soft clay a few weeks ago? We got too much water in it, and some of the children would have nothing to do with the clay, but not Leslie. She thought it was just fine.

Jane: And I think one of us fishes her out of the fountain or the bathroom lavatory, with soapsuds up to her elbows, nearly every Sunday. Is that part of the same messing around business?

Harriet: Most children love to mess around, don't they?

Ellen: None of the others do as much of it as Leslie does.

Jane: I never have to get anyone else out of the bathroom up to his or her ears in soap and the floor running with water.

Alice: Certainly lots of children do like to mess around, as we've been calling it, and there's good reason for it. Working with some material that you can control, that you can bend to your will, and no one says "nay" or "it doesn't look like anything," is very relaxing activity. It provides release from tension. The child forgets everything else in the engrossing activity of creating something with his hands — even a sink full of soapsuds — and when he's finished he sometimes feels almost tired. Then he would like you to do something with him, or for him, like reading a book. Leslie has spent some time each Sunday in some such activity as this, and I think that it's been a real help to her. She's more relaxed, and she plays more creatively for longer periods of time with whatever activity she has chosen.

Using Records in Learning How to Teach

How do teachers learn to teach by studying anecdotal records? How do you use such records at a teachers' meeting?

First, assemble the records in the order in which the recorded events have taken place. If one teacher can compile these and before the meeting make a copy of them for each of the teachers, the records will be studied more easily. If this cannot be done, each teacher in turn can read her records to the group while one teacher lists the episodes by date on a blackboard or large sheet of paper with a key word or phrase from each episode.

Second, talk about the record, beginning at whatever point the teachers determine. New understandings and increased awareness of what the teachers do not understand always come out of such thoughtful discussion.

Third, summarize the evening's work by writing down specific statements, such as:

A. A description of the child: what he likes to do and what he apparently does not enjoy doing; his relationship with the other children; his particular friends in the group, if any; how he handles anger, disappointment, frustration, and so forth.

B. What the teacher should and should not say and do with this child. The evening's discussion should offer some clues of what the child's needs are, what his most pressing developmental tasks are. These statements about the teacher's behavior will, of course, be deduced from these clues.

The teachers will find it aids their thinking and growing if they write these statements down in their journals. This record will serve as a reminder for the next few Sundays, and when kept during teachers' meetings throughout the year will provide much satisfaction and a real sense of accomplishment.

Alice, Jane, Ellen, and Harriet spent nearly forty minutes setting down some specific statements at the close of their evening's work.

A. About Leslie

1. Leslie seems to enjoy most (is most relaxed, absorbed, spends most time doing) clay, pasting, soap painting, water play.

She has worked at one puzzle only once in three months, and she listened to a story with other children once.

Her play is more manipulative than imaginative. (She rolls, pounds, squishes clay, rather than talking about it as she plays with it.)

2. Leslie seems happy, likes to come to church school, is not fearful, shy, retired. She has engaged occasionally in creative play with another child. More often she has entered into another's play by disrupting it (threw dishes, upset doll beds, knocked down blocks).

3. We have not seen her angry, sulking, suffering hurt feelings, crying. Reprimands from the teachers, or her mother, or hits and loud rebukes from other children seem not to affect her, unless it is to make her grin more impish.

B. What I, The Teacher, Should Do:
(The clue is that Leslie needs to feel accepted here by teachers and children. She needs to feel that she is not " bad.")

1. When Leslie is " up in the air " (throwing, upsetting, disrupting) offer her clay, paste, soap or finger paint, soap and water play, OR

2. Join her in play with the toys she's misusing and in such a way that she has a good time with them and with me, and perhaps with two or three other children (such as the tea party episode), OR

3. If someone else is playing with the toys she has misused, help her restore the damage and stay with her *until* she's happily at play again.

4. Observe and carefully record the incidents in which I (the teacher) did something that was good with Leslie, her big sister, or any child. Remember particularly my feelings at the time. Try to understand in recording the incident why I felt the way I did.

By working with anecdotal records over a period of some months, teachers will come to hold some important convictions about children and will become increasingly sensitive to them and understanding of them. Teachers will know that a child's behavior is always a response to some experience or inner condition that the teacher may or may not be able to understand. They will be aware that even episodes that seem trivial are significant in providing an understanding of what the child is like and how the teacher should respond. They will understand that play is the business of the three-year-old, it is the way he grows and learns, that there is good reason for each piece of equipment and each kind of creative play material in the three-year-old room. Teachers will become more accepting of children and more competent in helping them express their feelings and solve their problems. And last, but perhaps most important in the growth of teachers, they will begin to understand themselves. They will begin to be aware of their feelings toward each child as well as of their actions. They will become more and more objective about how they really are treating the children and why. They will discover that learning some things about one's self is equally as important as learning some things about children — perhaps even more important.

Learning to Write Anecdotal Records
Increases a Teacher's Sensitivity

The meeting in which the teachers studied the anecdotal records on Leslie was very rewarding. In the weeks that followed, they came to feel that they had a very haphazard understanding of most of the other children in the room. Some of the teachers had made some observations, others had noticed different, even opposite things, and the teachers also had some questions about themselves. So each teacher decided to write some records of her own.

At the next meeting they talked about this and after considering all the children in the group, they chose four. Then the teachers looked again at the records on Leslie and developed some points to keep in mind when writing their own.

1. Avoid statements that are interpretations by the teacher. Instead, write exact accounts of what took place. To write " she made herself right at home," without going on to say exactly what she did that gave the teacher that idea, would be interpretative, judgmental. Such statements are of little value when the records are studied as a whole, for the reader has to accept the judgment of the writer without any supporting evidence for or against the judgment.

2. Write exactly what happened: who was there, what they were doing, what each one said, and how it ended. What seems like a really little episode on Sunday morning may take several pages to record accurately. Some of these details may seem insignificant in any one incident, but they are discovered to be important when a group of records made over a period of time is studied.

3. It is important to record the feelings of children as well as their actions. But to record the feelings of another always involves interpretation on the part of the teacher. Instead of writing, "Alan was enjoying himself," a better way would be to write, "Alan seemed to enjoy himself, for he didn't see or hear anything that went on around him, not even when Jimmy pulled his (Alan's) favorite squeaky wagon loaded with blocks right past him. Alan's face was relaxed; he looked pleased as he was working. Finally he looked at me and said, ' Look, I made a bird's nest!' " In other words, write the interpretation of the feeling plus all the supporting evidence that led to that interpretation.

4. Avoid using adjectives to describe a child, as, " Henry is a lazy child." Instead, write the whole episode which seemed to indicate his laziness, and let the reader make his own interpretation. In the light of later episodes, the original hunch of laziness may turn out to be quite wrong.

5. Record carefully and as objectively as you can what you did, what you said, how you felt, and how you think your behavior affected what happened. Here, too, avoid using adjectives without supporting evidence. Write the whole episode in as much detail as possible.

6. Every episode of every record must be considered strictly confidential. It is easy, in casual or social conversation, to relate unthinkingly " a funny little thing that happened in Sunday school last Sunday." Such things seem harmless enough, but they are likely to be misunderstood, misinterpreted, enlarged, repeated, and actually become a barrier to a good relationship between a teacher and a child and his family.

Teachers Grow in Their Commitment
as They Discuss Their Goals in Teaching

The teachers of the three-year-old group felt, after these evenings spent with records, that there was still much to learn about the total job of teaching in a church school. In the transcribed records that follow, the teachers evaluated some of their recent experiences with the children, discussed their goals for teaching, and their own responsibilities to the children.

Ellen: I've always liked Leslie. I've always thought, "Well, she may act like that," but when I speak to her softly she always looks at you with such a grateful look in her eyes. Remember last Sunday when I was reading to Mitchell and Kathy, she just came very softly and sat by my side, and she sat there a little while? Then just as suddenly she walked away as much as if to say, "I guess I'm not interested after all," but after a while she did come back, didn't she?

Alice: Then what happened? I'm very curious.

Harriet: Well, let's see. What did happen? She was playing with clay, was that it? And then she went out to the fountain to wet the clay, was that it? No, it was to wash her hands. She kept going out of the room to wash her hands and get drinks, and I kept my eye on her, from your clue about her love of water at our last meeting, and she seemed to be doing fine, so I left her, for maybe two minutes. And it happened! She was soaked to her elbows. And I thought, "Oh, what will her mother say?" Really, I guess the last ten minutes were not very satisfying. Leslie just didn't know what to do with herself.

Alice: And what understanding do you have for this?

Harriet: I don't know really, except that she was sort of getting at loose ends, but that's not really an insight . . .

Alice: It seems as though she had sort of run down on finding her own way around, and she needed someone to take her by the hand and lead her to something, or maybe do it right along with her. . . . Could that have been it?

Harriet: Yes, that might have been the solution. It was so close to the end and Ellen, you were reading, and I was doing the clay . . .

Ellen: Yes, we were all busy and . . .

61

Harriet: And we were all busy, I suppose; none of us really noticed.

Alice: There's a pretty good psychological reason why the beginning of the hour — and for nursery children perhaps forty to fifty minutes of the hour (we really have an hour and a half, don't we?) — should be child-directed activity, and that's why we have all the equipment we have, and why the room is set up before the children come. Older children can participate in group activity and in teacher-directed activity, but most of our children can't. Betsy decides she'll play with dishes today, and Alan decides to load the little wagon with blocks, and Kathy and Henry go to do puzzles. Each one can come in, look the room over, and find what he wants to do. It is also true that these children *do* run down.

Harriet: In fact, now I remember, the whole group ran down about that time.

Alice: They get to the point where the children just can't find another thing *they* want to do. They don't know *what* they want to do.

Jane: That's why the story and songs and finger plays are so good then. I've been learning a few from TV that I thought we could use at the end of the hour to make things a little happier.

Harriet: We had planned to do this on Sunday, hadn't we, Ellen?

Ellen: Yes, we had, but . . .

Harriet: But the children were all so busy and so happily engaged when the time came that we decided not to interrupt it and put things away.

Ellen: And it was all a mistake.

Harriet: It sure was, for it wasn't five minutes before it all fell apart, and it was quite hectic just at the end there.

Harriet: I had another funny experience I didn't understand. . . . Remember the Sunday when there were just a few there, and Leslie tipped over the whole dish cupboard and spilled all the dishes on the floor? I insisted she pick them up, and she would have nothing to do with this, so I made her sit on the piano bench until she was ready to pick them up, and then she could come and play. She sat there and sat there and sat there, for fifteen minutes, I bet. And every few minutes I'd ask her if she wanted to pick up the dishes with me now, and she said, "No." Finally, a long time later, she came with me and picked up about two dishes, and I did the rest.

I was amazed at how she reacted to it. She didn't try to get off, and I wondered if I were doing the right thing. She didn't fuss or play the piano or anything.

Alice: Early in October I had the same experience with Leslie, with the same reaction on my part, I remember.

Harriet: Maybe this is a common form of discipline with her.

Jane: But still, why didn't she rebel? She rebels at other things; why not this?

Alice: Leslie is an interesting child. . . . I doubt if she really rebels against discipline in any overt manner. I think she rebels by doing the same thing again when her mother isn't looking. . . .

. . . I'm not sure that sitting Leslie on a chair is good discipline for her. Nonetheless, we can't overlook this helter-skelter activity that is disruptive, throwing things around, knocking apart another child's road or building.

Jane: What do you do or say?

Alice: I usually try to let the child, who has knocked the thing down, know just how the other child feels. "Jamie has worked quite hard on this garage and just about had it finished, and now he feels quite bad and even angry that you have knocked it down." The trespasser may never have thought of such a thing.

Jane: Perhaps you should suggest to Leslie — or whoever — that she could help Jamie rebuild something that's a part of what was knocked down, like making a road to the garage.

Alice: That's a possibility . . . if Jamie wants her to.

Harriet: That's a good point. George, my son, gets furious when that happens to him, and he never wants any help to fix it up.

Jane: I think I may as well be honest with you girls. I really wonder if I'm cut out for this sort of thing, because I think that all of this adds up to exactly no good. This may shock you, but I think I should say it, and if you don't think I belong here, you can find someone else.

Harriet: Oh, no!

Jane: I mean it, really. I don't think I have the right attitude. I know what children need, and I try to do the right thing with my own children. I realize you probably have a different attitude with other people's children, but I'm a firm believer that what goes on at home is really the important thing, and these little monsters that rule the roost are just going to be troublemakers no matter what, and one hour on Sunday isn't going to make one darn bit of difference. I'm a firm believer of that!

Alice: You think that's true.

Jane: And my idea of going into the group in the first place was just to get through the hour so the children don't kill one another and are reasonably happy until their mothers come back to get them. Now I obviously have the wrong attitude.

Harriet: Don't you think that you can see enough change in Leslie to show that it isn't entirely true?

Jane: Do you think it's making any difference to Leslie at *home?*

Harriet: I don't think it affects her whole behavior . . .

Jane: That's what I mean.

Harriet: But if she has this experience just once a week, it makes some difference to *her* . . . I don't think it will change her whole future, but for one thing, it will affect her relationship to the church.

Jane: That's an attitude I didn't think of.

Harriet: For the first time she's had a happy experience at church, and that's something.

Jane: Fine, but that just takes care of one aspect of her life, church school. She likes it there, so she won't rebel there. But in the meantime, she rebels against her home, against school — because she obviously won't get the individual attention there which you girls are trying to give her here, and so she'll keep coming to church, but what *difference* have you made in her *life?* Will it make any difference in her personality, really? Basically, she'll be doing the same things she's doing at home, and I just don't feel that one hour a week does anything for her.

Harriet: That may be. We have to accept our limitations. We have only one hour a week, and we have to do the best we can with it, and we can't expect to remake the lives of these children.

Jane: But you are, or else what's the point?

Harriet: We're trying to understand them, to help them as much as we can in this time. Let me put it this way. As a parent, it's tremendously important to me — in fact whether my child goes or not depends on it — whether he has a happy time in a group, whether there's a group where he fits in and is liked . . .

Jane: And the teacher is important there.

Harriet: And another reason our group is so important is that for many of the children this is their first group experience away from their mother and away from home. And the fact that this is in the church, and we are representatives of the church — I think in lots of ways we are helping the children form some very basic attitudes both toward the church and toward their future group relationships. More basic here than in the upper grades where they've already got . . .

Jane: But the problem is Leslie's home. If her mother knew what we were trying to do and could help, I think we could go one step further than I do now. I want to make Leslie reasonably happy here, too, but I don't think we can do much more than that because the problem is her family. They're the ones who need help. I don't think the child will get *anywhere* until the mother has someone to sit and talk with her for an hour a week. Do you see the point?

Alice: But it is true that every child — and every adult, too — needs some help in some direction at some time, and we just might be the person on hand who, by saying the right thing or being the right kind of person, will offer the child a new insight into his life or his relationships, or give him a new tool for handling a situation which before had completely perplexed and baffled him. Can't we do this?

Jane: Maybe we can. Of course, Leslie comes every Sunday and that's in our favor; but the ones who come once a month, what can you do? I began to teach because I felt someone had taken care of my children, and I have an obligation to help with other people's, but I think that for the time we spend thinking and planning for church school, the dividends are pretty low. It isn't worth it. Not that I don't enjoy it. I do immensely. I love getting together with you girls and talking it over. I just don't think it pays off.

Harriet: But we must be doing something good. I had Leslie all last year, and I tried to do with her the best I knew, Sunday after Sunday, and I felt that I had done nothing by the end of the year. Here it is January and she's a much different child than she was in October. *Something* has happened.

Alice: There's another aspect of this thing we haven't discussed. The Christian Church has believed, since its beginning, that its gospel of love, its way of living with love toward everyone, even one's enemies, can be taught to other people. This was a revolutionary idea in the Roman empire and even in the Jewish law, which allowed for revenge. The church believes that love can be communicated in such a way that people can learn to live in love. There may be some difference of opinion about the age at which this can happen, but the whole reason for the church's life and activity is to make love real in the lives of men.

We know that children learn to love by being loved. They learn to understand the feelings of others by having the people about them try to understand theirs. And children learn to forgive errors and thoughtless behavior by experiencing forgiveness of their own mistakes.

We are social beings who need love in order to live. We need to feel accepted by the people about us and to feel worth while in the life of society. If we don't feel this way, we become queer, and we contribute little to the service of men or of God.

In a world as wounded and scarred and as precarious as our present one is, we need our children to grow up feeling loved and capable of extending love. The nursery department of the church school can and should provide some of these experiences for children.

Jane: Perhaps it can do some, but the home *really* has to do it. I can't assume that big a responsibility for other people's children. I have enough responsibility for my own.

Alice: Long ago the Jewish people wrestled with that problem, too. God asked Cain where Abel was, and Cain responded, "Am I my brother's keeper?" The answer was yes. The Christian Church believes this, too. We are our brothers' keepers. I do feel responsible for those children I see every Sunday, and I keep wondering if I'm doing the best that can and should be done for them.

Jane: Really, I guess I agree with you. What's all this discussion about? (laughing)

Alice: I think the discussion is about the extent to which we can carry this responsibility. How do you make love operative when Leslie upsets all the dishes? We know not to condemn, pass judgment, express shock, but what do you do?

Jane: I guess I just don't have the same standards. I'll teach the children to do things with their hands and keep them from killing each other, but their emotional welfare doesn't bother me. I treat them like my own. If they get anything out of it, fine. If not . . . well?

Harriet: Children need good discipline, though, for discipline is a form of love. It shows them you care enough to be concerned about how they are acting. I felt that the chair sitting had no effect. Leslie learned nothing, not even that I cared about her . . . or least of all, that.

Another Important Area of Study
Is the Curriculum Material

Nursery teachers grow and learn by studying all the curriculum material developed for their age group: the quarterlies and the textbooks they are using, the supplementary materials found in the fifteen and twenty-five cent storybooks, other books for children, children's song books, books of prayers for children, and so on. The written material — stories, songs, prayers — as well as the activity or project material and the guidance material for the church school program can be critically evaluated by teachers with great personal benefit to them and to their groups. Through such a study the teachers will come to understand the material better, how it should best be used, why it is written the way it is. And they will understand the general or " average " characteristics of the nursery child better.

Here are some suggested criteria for evaluating and studying materials planned for the nursery department of the church. These criteria can be used in different ways. Each teacher may do some " homework " before a meeting, using a copy of these criteria and some specific piece of material. The results of this individual study are then shared and discussed when the teachers meet together. Or as a group, the teachers may analyze and evaluate some material and then each do individual work with one chosen piece of curriculum material.

Criteria for Evaluating and Studying Curriculum Materials

1. Does this piece of material, or activity, or project take into account what we know about the developmental picture of the nursery age child? —

    a. His vocabulary.

b. His sense of time and distance.

c. His attention span.

d. His world of people, places, ideas, and interests.

e. His ability to deal with abstract ideas.

f. His physical skills. (Can *he* do it or must the teacher?)

g. His identification with the HERE and NOW; his tendency to consider LONG AGO and FAR AWAY unreal

2. Does this material, or activity, or project have meaning for him? Is it something real, important, related to the world as he knows the world? Does it grow out of his experience, his wonderings? Does it provide for him a new understanding, or an interpretation? Can it be an expression of his own creative spirit?

OR is it something put on top of him, something pleasant enough but actually irrelevant to his life, " memory work " that he forgets as soon as it is over, or " busywork " that he leaves in the car when he goes into the house?

3. Do the words and the ideas implied in this material or activity — assuming they are understandable to the child — fit our beliefs? Are the ideas ones that can be enlarged to fit the child's growing understanding, that do not have to be unlearned at any point — grade school, high school, college, or adulthood? (For in the unlearning the child may throw out the whole church school experience.)

Using the Material in Planning the Program

Teachers often use the curriculum material provided for them as a step by step outline for the Sunday morning's activity. It can be used this way, but it doesn't have to be. Probably most Sunday mornings in most churches the curriculum material should not be. Curriculum material is for the guidance of the teacher. It offers suggestions and interpretations, and provides some resources for each Sunday. It has its greatest value when it is adapted by each teacher to suit her skills, her nursery room, and her children.

Alice Todd and her teachers were working out some plans for three or four Sundays in spring.

Ellen: Our nursery teacher's guide suggests that we take a walk, but I think that's a poor idea for us in this city. The children couldn't see anything sprouting or budding. The boulevard trees are too tall, the grass is all walked on, and we would be so busy watching that no child got into the street, that we couldn't stop to look at anything.

Harriet: That's right, and Trixie is afraid of dogs. I saw her run crying up the steps to the church in a perfect panic this morning because she saw a dog at the corner.

Alice: What can we do then so the children can see for themselves that what seemed dead is coming alive?

Jane: We could plant marigold seeds in little pots right in our room and let each child take his home and take care of it. If they can't set the plant out later, it might even bloom in the window of the apartment.

Harriet: I bet it would. We ought to be sure each child plants about four seeds just in case.

Ellen: We ought to do that pretty late in the spring so the plant won't be too large to set out, shouldn't we?

Alice: We should have some stories of spring on hand both for telling and for the book table. Do you know any?

Harriet: Last year my children enjoyed Lois Lenski's book, *Spring Is Here.* We got it from the public library, and I could get it again for two Sundays.

Alice: And I remember a book I used some years ago, *The Wind and Peter.* Harriet, could you look up that one, too?

Ellen: I know, let's make kites one windy Sunday if we have one. The paper bag kites it tells about in the book would be easy and fun for the children. I'll have the supplies here, so when the right Sunday comes we can do it — as many children as want to.

Jane: I'll change the bulletin board pictures. I came across a beautiful picture of a mother bird looking at some eggs in her nest last week. It would be appropriate.

Ellen: (laughing) I bet she wasn't looking at them. . . . Surely we will have some rain one Sunday — or maybe on a Saturday — that we could make use of somehow.

Jane: If it's on a Saturday, it won't be much good. Three-year-olds wouldn't get much understanding of Saturday's rain on a sunny Sunday, would they?

Ellen: No. I guess not. Anyway, if it rains on a Sunday we could sing, "It's Raining." What else could we do?

Harriet: How about playing, "Oats, Peas, Beans and Barley Grow"? That's about growing and seeds and sun and rain. The children could take turns being the farmer, and so forth.

Jane: I don't think that's so good with three-year-old children. They can't wait for turns. They'll all want to be farmers, or the sun or whatever. That's for the kindergarten, isn't it?

Alice: I think it would be more fun for five-year-olds, but we could use the song, sing it to the children as we plant our marigold seeds, or use it following one of our springtime stories. Only we ought to change the words. It doesn't make much sense to sing about oats, peas, beans and at the same time be planting marigolds. How about singing "Little seeds to flowers grow"?

A teacher by herself — or teachers working together — will find Sunday morning in the nursery department most fun and least hectic if the planning is both careful and flexible. Teachers need to have stories, songs, ideas, creative materials ready for use before the session starts. But these materials may not be used. The weather may make the plans inappropriate; Joan may show by her behavior that she would profit more from the story of "The New Baby" than from "Helping at Home"; or Johnny's turtle may provide much better conversation material than the baby rabbit picture. The skilled teacher uses the experiences of the morning for the Sunday program, knowing that living and growing and learning are all of a piece. Oftentimes, however, nothing particularly new or interesting comes up. Then she uses what she has planned and introduces something new — a story, a song, an activity, or perhaps all three. It does not matter whether a plan was used or not. What matters is that the materials were available for use, if they had been needed.

Teachers Grow by Planning Together

There is a way for teachers to work together so that they grow in skill and adequacy and self-understanding. This way is more than a set of rules on how to have a good discussion or a collection of techniques on how to make meetings lively or interesting. The clue is the quality of the relationship that exists among the teachers themselves. Teachers grow in skill and understanding, in their ability to love and respond to and serve children — to treat children as persons — by being treated as persons themselves. The facts about children, the theories of personality development, the principles of good education — all these teachers learn quickly and most eagerly in a group relationship in which each one feels herself to be needed, worth while, a significant, contributing member, accepted as such by each of the other teachers.

Such feelings only become a real part of the atmosphere at a teachers' meeting or on Sunday morning when *all* the teachers work together as a team. This means the teachers make decisions *together* concerning their Sunday program, their teachers' meetings (when and where and content), schedules, home visits, and any other matters that concern the nursery department. Action taken is joint action; responsibility is shared.

As with children, so it should be with teachers; nothing is put down on top of them. As a group they formulate their own questions, clarify their own needs, discover their own answers. Each one is free to do her own growing in the direction she chooses to go. The role of the teacher-trainer is to be the helper along the way. Among these teachers each one is an " I " who thinks of every other one as a " Thou." This is a relationship of persons to persons. None is superior, none is inferior, each is unique, necessary, of great value to the total group.

How Teachers May Learn

Teachers learn in many ways: by studying anecdotal records and learning to write them; by evaluating their own recent experiences; by exploring their reasons for teaching and their responsibilities to the children and the church; by trying to establish some goals for the nursery class; by evaluating curricula; by planning together; by working with skilled Christian teachers; by attending laboratory schools and workshops.

Though mentioned here last, laboratory schools and workshops should come first in the training program that a board of Christian education or church school superintendent or department director makes available to teachers. The laboratory schools and workshops, which run for a week or more, may help a teacher gain more skills and grow more deeply in her Christian commitment and understanding than an entire year of teachers' meetings.

These are some of the methods. There are others equally as good. The critical factor in any method is the intangible quality of the human relationships among the people using the method. That we have said before. The way teachers, or anyone, learn to be real persons, actively involved in growing toward Christian maturity, is in a relationship with other persons who are consciously, and with great excitement, going the same path, in pursuit of the same goal.

FOR YOU TO THINK ABOUT

1. In order to discover how much they knew about one child in the class and how clearly and exactly they thought about her, the teachers composed a sample anecdotal record together.

" One child I've particularly noticed is little Clara. She's so tiny and so sweet. All the Sundays she's been coming she's never given any child any reason to contradict her or anything. She's such a sweet child.". . . " She looks about one and a half; she's really three and a half." . . . " Somehow I've always liked Clara. Of course, I've found out she doesn't quite do things on her own; you have to kind of lead her. You ask her, would she like to paste — Oh, yes, that would be agreeable; would she like to play with clay — Yes, that would be agreeable with her. Anything she does she seems to do well.". . . " I've noticed she likes the dishes and the doll corner. She plays there a lot; maybe it's because she's familiar with those things, knows how to do things with them. She's not an aggressive child; if she were she would not go for the thing she had done before.". . . " I think she's a little younger, if not chronologically, in other ways. She is so tiny, at least she gives you that impression. . . ."

 a. Find the statements that are interpretations without supporting evidence.

 b. List the things you know for sure about Clara from this record. List the statements which require careful anecdotal records in order to be valuable to a teacher's understanding of Clara.

 c. Teachers often try to find reasons for vague impressions they have about a child before they check the accuracy of their impressions. Find the illustrations of this in the above " record."

2. Keep a journal of " Success Stories." Enter any episode in which something you said or did proved to be particularly helpful to a child. After a month or two, look back over the accounts and try to discover why these were good experiences. Did they help a child understand himself or some other person better? or save face? or gain a new sense of adequacy?

3. From the record, see page 62, would you say that sitting Leslie on a chair was good discipline? Why or why not? What is the purpose of discipline?

4. How could Alice Todd have treated Leslie's sister so that she felt accepted and yet know that she was not to be hovering over the nursery room?

5. How about planning your teaching by quarters? At the beginning of a quarter assemble all the stories, play materials, activity ideas, and so forth, which you feel might be useful on some Sunday morning during that quarter. Keep these in your teacher's cupboard so that when the day for planting crocuses, for example, arrives, your story and pictures will be ready. You'll have your ideas marked and within reach on whatever Sunday they are needed.

6. How do you feel about Jane's point of view that the Sunday morning nursery program is really very insignificant in the difference it can make to a child's religious development?

CHAPTER FIVE

The Religious Foundation of the Nursery Program

AT THIS POINT we must consider a very pertinent question. Granted that the nature of children is as has been described here, and that an understanding of the growth of personality toward Christian maturity is necessary for setting up a church school program for nursery children and for the training of leaders, what is *Christian* about all this? Do not the really wise and creative educators and school systems base their programs on these two concepts: the nature of the child being taught, and a theory of how he grows and learns? Yes, some do, and the results are outstanding. We wish all children could be part of such a school system with such wise and understanding teachers. But there is a dimension to the educational process here described that is peculiarly Christian, a motivation that may exist in secular education but is very probably not verbalized.

The motivation is love. Establishing this kind of relationship with a child is the way to love him. Showing love to all men is the life to which we have been called. This is the gospel we teach and preach and try to practice. Christianity is not just a set of ideas about the nature of God, how he is at work in the world, and how men should act. Nor is it just a way of living with kindness and thoughtfulness. Much of the emphasis in leadership training sessions and the activity of our church school classes centers around Christian ideas and facts, almost on the assumption that if a teacher or pupil learned enough about the traditions and the ideas of Christianity, he or she would thereby become a good Christian.

On the other hand, it is not enough just to like children, to be "a good guy" with the boys or popular with the girls. Christianity as a way of living is not merely easygoing, friendly, harmonious relationships with all people. No, the love proclaimed by Jesus is more hard-hitting, more difficult than that. It is to extend oneself in persistent active concern for another, no matter what his condition of body or spirit, though he be most unlovable, though he reject and mock and spit upon your service or your thoughtfulness. It is to seek to understand him, always to accept him, repeatedly to forgive him. This is the nature of the love that saves men from their own greed and hate and self-concern, and is the only love that will redeem the world from strife and possible destruction. Christianity is not just ideas, nor just " sweetness and light." It is a unity of thought and action in which the love of God proclaimed by Jesus, and demonstrated by Jesus' life as we read about it in the Bible, becomes the basis of the relationship between people here and now.

How is the kind of teaching herein described an expression of love for a child? It is one human being serving another human being when and where he has need. Most teachers do this easily and without much thought in the areas of the physical and the intellectual life. We help the child to tie his shoes, undo the hard knots, get on his snowpants, hitch the car to the truck; and we help him learn to fit the puzzle piece in place, what the names of the colors are, how to identify two or three or four objects.

In other areas of growth — social, emotional, psychological, religious — we are not so skilled in offering help, for we do not see so clearly what the child's need is. We do not know the various meanings that underlie his behavior, so we brand him with some adjectives, and start dealing with him from the point of view this brand implies. This one is a sweet child, that one is "ornery," another is lazy, or a crybaby, or shy. Thinking of a child in such words as these adds one more handicap to our understanding of him and really *loving* him; and by loving him, we mean offering him the kind of help he needs or being to him the kind of person he needs.

Let us illustrate this. One Sunday Jimmy had three or four tearful moments. Somebody stepped on his finger; another child took the red crayon he was going to use; he could not find his favorite book on butterflies that he read each Sunday; and finally, his hat was gone from his hook when it was time to go home. Jimmy's emotional distress seemed to the teacher to be greater than the trouble warranted. His finger was not really hurt; there were several other red crayons in the box; the book turned up on the other end of the table; and his hat was found lying on the floor underneath the hook. Besides, it was not like Jimmy to be disturbed over such trivial matters. What was wrong with Jimmy; what did he need; what should the teacher do?

She could point out to him that the trouble was really not a bad one, and all he needed to do was to brush off the finger, find another crayon, or look a little harder for the butterfly book and his hat. She could treat each situation with as much seriousness as he was treating it — bandage the reddened finger, understand how disappointing it was not to be able to use the crayon he was planning to use or to read the book he wanted, berate the hat for falling on the floor. She could probably do many other things.

What she *should* do depends upon what meaning she can discover behind his behavior. Does he have a new baby at home? Have his parents taken a vacation and left him with a trusted housekeeper? Has he had some great fear or has someone he knew well died? The only safe assumption this teacher can make from one Sunday's experience like this is that this behavior is a signal of distress. Jimmy needs help. To show love to Jimmy at this point is to extend to him exactly the kind of help he needs.

How to do this? Each teacher will do it differently, depending upon her experience and understanding. She may read to discover all the possible reasons for this behavior; she may study her past anecdotal records to see what clues they offer; she almost certainly will visit his home or talk with his mother on the telephone; she may consult with her minister either to see if he knows of troubles in Jimmy's home or to inform him that there may be some.

This kind of effort consumes both time and energy, and doing what is needful for a child under stress is often emotionally exhausting as well. Loving another, desiring for him wholeness and fullness of life, and spending yourself to help him find that kind of life is not easy, and it is not a one-hour-on-Sunday-morning proposition. Such work has the qualities of an honest and sincere prayer of intercession, for it is not a vague " bless Jimmy, who seems to be unhappy," but it is rather seeking to discover what good thing does need to happen to or for Jimmy, and then going to work to cause it to happen. This method of teaching — of establishing a loving relationship with each child — is one way of living a Christian life.

Such a relationship as this grows directly out of another Christian doctrine: the value of persons. We believe that man is created in the image of God, that there is something of the Divine Creator within him. Therefore, personality is sacred; human life is valuable. Because man is, he is of intrinsic worth. That which serves life, develops its skills, conserves health, offers freedom to body and spirit is Good; that which preys upon life, injures health, warps personality, restricts the free development of mind or body is Evil and sinful. The relationship that exists between two people, both created in the image of God, can be good or evil. The relationship here described as the basis for Christian teaching is one in which each person thinks more highly of the other than he does of himself; he enjoys the other, respects the other, serves the other. He treats him as a person, a " Thou," a child of God; and he thinks of himself in the same terms. This is a relationship of persons, brothers, equals in the eyes of God, each of whom serves the other's need before his own. It is good.

This Relationship of Love Introduces the Child to Some of the Basic Experiences of Christian Living

There comes a time when the child wants to know more about God, where he lives, what is he like, what does he do? These are difficult questions to answer in such a way that the child will have any more understanding than he had before the questions were asked. If the child has experienced love and trust, understanding and forgiveness, and has heard and used these words in connection with the experiences he has had, he will have some understanding of what is meant by the Christian conviction that "God is Love." *These virtues* or qualities of human life *partake of the nature of God*, and although none of us knows the *All* of the nature of God, still, we can have some understanding of God if we have had some of these experiences. Without them and without the words for them, there would be no understandable way to describe God to a child.

Likewise, *he can begin to understand Jesus* as kind, loving, forgiving, accepting of all people in all conditions, if the child has had some experience with the attitudes and feelings these words describe. If, when you use these words, you have the feelings to which these words refer, if the young child has felt these feelings coming from others to him and going out from himself toward others, then the life of Jesus will begin to have meaning for him.

A child who experiences the kind of loving relationship with a teacher which we have just described, has a *beginning experience of the Christian fellowship — the Church*. The attitude of his teacher about the kind of person she must be, and about the nature of the religious task she is undertaking, conveys to the child a sureness about the kind of people who are in the church. They like you the way you are; they'll help you when you need it; they understand when you feel bad; and they help you become what you want to be without judging you or condemning you. This is the Church which is the body of Christ, and children who have good church school experiences are on the way to emotional identification with the people and the life of their church. "That is my church. I like to go there."

Can a child have an *experience of prayer* in this kind of church school program, or of the Bible? To have an experience of prayer or an experience with the Bible of the kind that renews your strength, reorients your thinking, provides new insights into the will of God for your life, clearly requires a maturity not possessed by three-year-olds. But a three-year-old can learn some things *about* prayer and *about* the Bible from his church experience, as well as from his home, and he can develop some positive attitudes toward prayer and the Bible, even if he does not have a complete understanding of either one.

A three-year-old by listening can participate in a quiet simple prayer that grows out of an immediate experience he has had, such as the " Thank You " prayer Mrs. Todd said that first Sunday morning after the story about doctors. Such prayers, sincerely spoken in words children use and understand, convey both a meaning and a feeling that is real to children. Of course, not every prayer every Sunday will mean something to every child. Just as children's abilities to listen to and understand stories vary greatly, so does their response to prayer. But when a child sees the grownups whom he knows and loves and who love him pray, whether he understands the whole of it or not, he comes to associate prayer with them, and prayer becomes part of his whole set of feelings about these people and the church. Likewise, grace at mealtime at home becomes so much a part of the family tradition that even the two-and-a-half-year-old will remind the family to say grace. And although he probably does not understand the gratitude for God's care expressed in the grace, the child accepts it as a significant something that the family does together.

Much the same thing can be said of the Bible. There are a few — very few — stories in it which are intellectually and emotionally suitable to the three-year-old, but the use of the Bible in his presence doesn't have to be limited to the reading or telling of these few stories. Watching his parents and his teachers hold the Bible, seeing them read it in quietness and meditation, assures him that it is an important book to them. He develops positive feelings toward it, wants to hold it for himself, looks forward to the day when he will have a Bible of his very own.

It is necessary to remember that growing in the Christian life follows a pattern as surely as does physical growth. We do not try to teach a child to walk before he can sit up. By the same token The Lord's Prayer is many, many steps beyond the few spoken words that arise out of the feeling and experience of the moment which is prayer for the three-year-old. There is an order to growth — any kind of growth — that will prevail in spite of our effort to short-circuit it. Trying to rush growth, or to take the steps out of order, often has the effect of confusing the present growing, and blunting the enthusiasm and exhilaration for what lies ahead. We must not, in our teaching, use words or ideas or symbols that the child can only misunderstand. If we do, he must unlearn strange notions and ideas before he can learn the right ones which we intended all along. This makes the process doubly hard for a child and for the teacher, and may make the ideas seem " old stuff " that has been heard before but never really experienced with understanding.

We do not have to teach the whole of the Christian faith and tradition and practice to the three-year-old. Let us remember what he is like. He — like all of us — really learns what he experiences, not what he hears about. Let us be sure that he is *experiencing* the Christian life.

FOR YOU TO THINK ABOUT

1. Select from your nursery class the child with whom you find it most difficult to deal. Try to work out an understanding of his behavior — what he is seeking to accomplish, what troubles him, what he is suffering. Then plan the kinds of experiences he needs that will help him.

2. Write a description in short sentences and with words three-year-olds use and understand of:

    a. God
    b. Jesus
    c. The Church
    d. The Bible
    e. Prayer

(This is for your own understanding, not for use with the three-year-olds.)

PART THREE

Visiting in the Home

". . . You shall love the Lord your God with all your heart, and with all your soul, and with all your mind. This is the great and first commandment. And a second is like it, You shall love your neighbor as yourself."

Matthew 22: 37b-39

Bear one another's burdens, and so fulfil the law of Christ.

Galatians 6: 2

CHAPTER SIX

The Home Call: The Personal Ministry of the Church to the Family

O NE OF THE ways a teacher and a child come to know each other better is through a home call or visit. Hardly a recent text-book or church school lesson quarterly neglects the suggestion that the teacher should visit the child's home either early in the church school year or at frequent intervals throughout the year. Many church school curricula, from nursery through high school, de-pend for their effectiveness on church-home co-operation in the matter of the child's religious education.

There is no argument that often very effective ministering results when someone from the church visits a family in its home. A home call is the genuine expression of the church's interest in and concern for persons, both parents and children; and as such, it is not only the rightful use of the church's " talents " (time, energy, leadership), but even more, it is one of its obligations.

Not enough calling is ever done. Most ministers feel that this is one of the great, never-to-be-finished tasks of their ministry. Most conscientious teachers feel a vague uneasiness when " home call " is mentioned, but they cannot quite get up enough courage to undertake a call. Most parents would feel pleased if the minister or church school teacher could get around to calling on them — in fact, some feel very neglected that they never have been called on. In many of our churches, it is not humanly pos-sible for the minister to call on all the members and friends of the church in addition to the calling that must be done on those who are sick, bereft, and in great trouble or crisis. Someone else, in the name of and with the concern of the church, has to help. This could be a lay person designated and trained as the church caller. It could be the teachers of the church school and should be.

Many teachers, when the discussion of making home calls comes up, begin to feel butterflies in their stomachs and their hands getting cold. "What would I do? What would I say? Why should I go in the first place? What if they don't want me to come — if it's the wrong time, or they don't want to be bothered? Goodness, it's a big enough job learning to be a good teacher, let alone becoming a church home visitor. Let someone else do it."

Someone else can, and in some churches someone else does. She is a nursery visitor representing the nursery department of the church. All families, including those expecting their first baby as well as those with children from infancy through three years of age, are her concern. Worked at regularly and spread over the year, this may not be an impossible task for one person. Some churches, however, are so large and the population with children in this age bracket is growing so fast, that one person cannot serve all these families. Clearly then, the responsibilities must be shared, and the teachers of the nursery children, *if* they have the qualifications, are the persons who can serve these families best. One way this can be done is to have a team of nursery visitors, three or four instead of one, to work with the nursery teachers of the church school in serving these families.

What is the purpose of a call? It is to establish a relationship between church and home. There is no one way to do this. If the nursery visitor approaches the members of the family with an attitude of wanting to know them, to enjoy them, and to become their friend, she most likely will succeed. If, after she has gone, the family feels that the church is interested in them and stands ready to include them in its fellowship and offer them help where it can, she has succeeded. It is not the words the visitor says so much as the feelings she has which are important. For what she says, how she listens, and how she responds, all spring from the feelings and attitudes she has about herself, her church, and other people.

84

The kind of call that develops may follow any one of four rather distinct patterns.

The call might be the *first contact* between the home and some person representing the church. It would be a time of " feeling out," and getting acquainted. The visitor would get to know the child or children of the family, or at least the vital statistics about them, and would see the family as a unit. The parents, and the other children, if present, would feel that the church is interested in them as persons and stands ready to be a genuine part of their lives.

The call might be an *informative conversation*. Parents often have many stored-up questions about the church that they have not bothered to ask the minister nor have they known whom else to ask. Is there a couples' club for us and when and where does it meet? Are there adult classes in the church school or on Sunday evenings or during the week? Are there parents' groups or clubs? What is the Christian education program of the church? What does the church believe, what does it teach, especially to our three-year-old? And a family new to the community may want to know various things about the resources and the services of the community as well as, " Who is the best dry cleaner or has the best meat? "

Other parents may want help and information on such matters as: how to carry on religious training at home; which religious practices to observe and how and when; what shall we do about family worship; and what should we be teaching our children about God and Jesus and the Bible? A call that develops into this kind of conversation, expressing such needs as these, usually means that the church visitor will need to call again with some concrete suggestions and some materials to give the family. She does not need to have a bag of tricks up her sleeve or the answer to every conceivable question in her head before she rings the bell. *The reason for her call is to express the church's desire to serve the family.* Whether she can perform the service herself in two or three calls, or whether she does not have all the skill or resources called for in a particular visit, in no wise indicates that she should not do the calling. No one, not even the minister, can perform every service and skill needed by some persons; but each of us can do something if we are willing to spend some time preparing and studying and practicing.

In no situation is this more true than in the call that really becomes a *counseling conversation*. This is the visit during which one parent, or both of them, finds an understanding person who knows how to listen while he or she — or they — talks out a problem that is personal, confidential, and very disturbing. Usually no one can predict when a call will take this direction, neither the caller nor the parents. It is probably true that the home visitor who has spent some time learning some skills for listening and responding to this kind of conversation will find himself, or herself, having more counseling conversations than the visitor who has no such skill or understanding.

A call that goes in this direction might well be unsettling or embarrassing to the nursery visitor. It is understandable that many teachers feel they can visit in the home as long as they do not have to deal with any personal problems in the family. Many teachers do not feel they have the skill, the understanding, the spiritual resources necessary to be of help. "This is the minister's job" they say.

True, it is. But a home visitor who succeeds in becoming a friend to the families of young children is, sooner or later, going to find herself listening to some kind of real and distressing family problems. She cannot at that point say, "Why don't you discuss this with Pastor Brown; I'm sure he could help you better than I can?" without, in effect, rejecting the family and cutting off the growth in friendship between the family and herself. A person usually shares his problems with someone whom he feels he can trust. Finding himself and his problem referred, no matter how skillfully, to another person makes him feel guilty for having trespassed against a friendship, or anxious that his problem may be worse than he at first thought, or disappointed and angry that the help the church offered was not its own but that of some welfare agency or counseling service.

This does not mean that the nursery visitor will be able to handle everything that comes to her. Persons who are very deeply disturbed need professional psychiatric help. The nursery visitor should refer such cases to her minister who may be able to aid the family in securing the help that is needed. But many of the personal problems the visitor will encounter will not be such deep personality disturbances that she cannot be of real help in dealing with them, if she will take the thought and time to learn some skills. The second half of this chapter describes how a teacher can do this.

The fourth kind of call is primarily a *discussion of the child* in the home. The parents may need someone just to listen to them talk about their child and enjoy him with them, or they may need specific information and help. Again, if the nursery home visitor does not have the particular help needed, and she may not if it is something that can be found in a book or pamphlet, she can always make an appointment to return at the parents' convenience with the material or the wisdom required. Young parents of a first child, particularly, are likely to find their lives more restricted than they had anticipated, and the little vexing problems that seem to have no answers are endless. The nursery home visitor who really knows and understands babies and young children can become a great support and a real friend to a new mother and father. Parents of kindergartners and school age children often have their own social groups through the school system that offer them understanding and encouragement. New parents are often alone with their babies for three or four years and really need someone to stand by them.

Some calls could have all of these aspects. Many calls will be composed of several of them. None of this matters, of course. Our concern is that the visit to the home by someone from the church be helpful and valuable to the family. Any home visit, whether it be with a family with their baby yet unborn or with their children in high school, has this same purpose. Only the subject matter is different.

What are the necessary qualifications of the person who is to do the home visiting for the nursery department? She must have the knowledge, skills, and understandings required to handle any one of the four courses a call might take:

1. She enjoys doing it, likes to meet and learn to know people,
   ... extends a warm personality that is friendly and tactful,
   ... is not prying, proselytizing, seeking finances,
   ... is offering herself, her friendship, her services to the family according to their needs.

2. She knows her church,
   ... how it is organized,
   ... its social and fellowship groups where each family member can fit,
   ... its religious education program, the philosophy and the curriculum, particularly for the babies through nursery age,
   ... how to find out what she does not know.
   AND her community, especially the service and welfare agencies.

3. She has learned some skills in *listening*,
   ... she listens with ears and mind and *heart*,
   ... she understands and responds with understanding,
   ... she knows the kind of responses not to make,
   ... she knows when the family needs skilled help and later refers the minister to them,
   ... she appreciates the confidential nature of *all* her calls.

4. She has a deep, genuine interest in children to the degree that she will learn, as part of her preparation for becoming the nursery home visitor, or has already learned, something of the developmental picture of a child from infancy through the pre-school years. She will be acquainted with such " problems " as thumb-sucking, head-banging, negativism, stuttering, regression in toilet training, and will know what the leading pediatricians and nursery school educators think about such problems. She will know what is " normal " in the development of children and be aware of the wide variations within the " normal." She will know something of the developmental sequence, the order or

pattern of growth, that is inherent in each child; and she will know that she does not know everything. Therefore, she will be able to recommend pamphlets and books that are helpful to parents of young children,[1] and she should know the name of a local physician or pediatrician whom she can recommend.

The nursery home visitor does not have to be a member of the teaching staff of the church school. However, if she is not, she should be an integral part of the work of the nursery department. She should know the teachers and attend teachers' meetings; she should know how the entire preschool department of the church school is organized and what its program is or is not for babies through five-year-olds.

If the nursery home visitor is one who has reared her family, she is in an excellent position to be of service. She will know from experience something of the trials and joys of living with and caring for young children " round the clock," something of the needs of the new family which faces new responsibilities in what may be their first home in a new community. She will understand that the parents may feel overworked, often they are; for the husband is trying hard to become a " success " for his family; there is a limited income which does not usually provide for week ends off from job or baby; and the parents' time may be so taken up it is difficult to cultivate friendships and establish social relationships within the new community.

The nursery home visitor also will know that some hours of the day she will be much more welcome than at other hours. In every case, a telephone call made ahead of time setting the hour for the call is a considerate thing to do. Because her family obligations are more or less flexible, she can easily fit her visiting into the convenience of the family.

On Sunday mornings the nursery home visitor will find that taking turns, by Sundays, visiting the rooms of the nursery department, if there is more than one, is valuable to her and to the families. By observing, she will come to know the children

---

[1] See p. 177 for a listing of some recommended materials.

better, and just being there to greet parents as they come and go may result in such conversations as: " When are you coming to see us again? " " I wish you had time to come back and talk with me some more about Charlie," or " We have a new neighbor with a three-year-old. I think they'd be interested in the church if someone like you could call on them." Thus she becomes the family's friend in the church school.

Anyone who makes visits in the homes in the name of the church is somewhat set apart by the community as the minister is. People begin to feel that they can trust her, that they can tell her anything they need to, that she will help them or find them help, and that *she will not betray their confidences*. She works closely with her minister, shares with him whatever information would be helpful for him to know, refers him to families whom he can help better than she. The home visitors of the church school and the minister thus become a team serving the families of the church in the name of Christ.

How does a teacher or a lay person learn how to make a call? That will be the concern of our next chapter. But here, a few brief suggestions about calling can be made.

1. For your own feeling of ease, have some reason for making the call besides the one of getting acquainted with the family. Take along a church school book, either the child's own copy which the family is to have, or the one written for the family if your curriculum materials are so designed; or a few pieces of worship material suitable for use with a three-year-old, such as graces at table, or suggestions for bedtime prayers; or some pertinent pamphlet material that may be helpful to parents of young children;[1] or an invitation to a parents' group or a family night at the church. This " thing in hand " may prove to be a real aid in becoming acquainted. On the other hand, the visit may be so animated that the " reason " may be almost completely forgotten. It does not matter. Material can be delivered and talked over at a

[1] Most denominations publish material of this type. Write to your denominational headquarters for further information. See also the listing on page 174 in the bibliography.

later visit, and an invitation to a meeting can be telephoned the next day.

2. Make an appointment with the family ahead of time, at their convenience, and when both parents can be present, unless the personal relationship between the visitor and the family is of such long standing that to call for an appointment would be laughable.

3. Keep always in mind that the call is to be of service to the family. Let them, not you, direct its course, determine its nature, although your sense of direction and knowledge of possible ways in which the church or particular people can be helpful will be needed.

The Counseling Conversation

A counseling conversation may also be called a creative conversation or a creative dialogue. It is talk between two or three persons (in the case below, the visitor and one parent) having qualities of significance, earnestness, honesty, love about it. The nursery visitor extends the warmth of her personality and the service of her church by listening and responding in something more than ordinary conversational patterns. And the parent, feeling the visitor's understanding and acceptance, is able to confront his problems and his feelings and begin to handle them, to grow through them.

Mrs. Todd had made an appointment with the mother and father of one of her three-year-olds, Ricky Scott. She arrived at the appointed time with the new quarter's nursery book under her arm and was greeted at the door by Mrs. Scott.

Mrs. Scott-1: I'm so glad you've come. I've been needing to talk to somebody. I don't know whether it will do any good or not, but I've been thinking about it ever since you called.

Mrs. Todd-1: I'm glad I came then, and if I can be of any help, I'd like to.

Scott-2: I'm sure anything will help at this point. Won't you sit down, Mrs. Todd? Let me take your coat. My husband regrets that he has had to make an unexpected out-of-town business trip and can't be here. He wanted me to change the appointment, but I've been looking forward to this since last week, and I felt too desperate to put it off.

Todd-2: You've really been upset.

Scott-3: We might not have been in such a state if we hadn't had to move when we did. My husband's work always seems to be an interruption just when we don't need an interruption. Mr. Gray, our minister, was such a help to us in Cherry Oaks, that if we hadn't had to leave when we did we might not be in such a state — at least Ricky might not.

Todd-3: You feel it's too bad you had to leave just when your minister was being so helpful.

Scott-4: Well, I guess that didn't make as much difference as I supposed. Tom says — he's my husband — it's not leaving Mr. Gray that did it, nor is his job the fault either. Maybe we had never really met the problem. Maybe we just thought we had.

Todd-4: Ummmmmmmmmmm.

Scott-5: I knew we needed some help, and I guess I should have come to the minister of your church for help, but I began to wonder if our last church was really helping very much. After we left Cherry Oaks it seemed to Tom and me that when the chips were down — when we really needed help — the church wasn't much good. They kept trying to buck us up, but they really couldn't give us the kind of help that stayed with us when we left.

Todd-5: Sometimes the help you got from your church seems superficial, and perhaps you're a little disappointed.

Scott-6: I guess I am. And Tom feels that the church is really nothing but nice-sounding words that don't do anyone any good but the preachers. Isn't that an awful thing to say?

Todd-6: After your experience you've come to wonder if the church isn't a lot of nice words that don't mean anything.

Scott-7: I don't know what to think at this point — but let me tell you what happened. You see, we had an older boy, Ronald, who would have been five last May, the same week that Ricky was three, but he was killed in February. He was on his sled and a car . . .

Todd-7: (Mrs. Scott cried quietly. Mrs. Todd responded by laying her hand on Mrs. Scott's arm in a gesture of friendship and said nothing.)

Scott-8: (She became more composed and went on.) We felt as though the world had ended at first, of course. And Ricky couldn't understand what had happened to Ronnie. We told him that Ronald had gone to live with God, that God needed him, and that seemed all right for a time. We slowly began to get hold of ourselves and decided not to be morbid or tearful and grieving in front of Ricky, and we tried to help him believe that life and death were all part of God's plan, and we couldn't understand everything about it. We thought we' believed it ourselves until we moved and then . . . (she began crying again) . . . everything fell apart.

Todd-8: All the hurt's still there, and the explanations you had worked out didn't hold up.

Scott-9: That's right. We moved here away from our friends and Ricky's. Tom began traveling all the time; Ricky began pulling out his hair and having crying spells and nightmares. He puts up such a fuss with a sitter — the last time I left him he was really distraught when I returned — so we don't go out until after he's asleep, and then we're never easy about it. He won't let me out of his sight — and I thought all this was because we moved. . . .

Todd-9: I see.

Scott-10: Then one day in one of his unhappy states he cried to me, "Why did God need Ronnie? Didn't he know I need him, too, to play with?" And I cried, too, all day long. (Mrs. Scott found it hard to talk.) I don't know the answer. It doesn't seem fair. He was such a little boy with such a love of life, and we all needed him and wanted him. What kind of God is it who'll allow little boys to be killed?

Todd-10: It's so hard to make sense out of it.

Scott-11: That's right, Mrs. Todd. Tell me what to think, what to tell Ricky. Tell me what is true!

Todd-11: You've got to find an answer for this experience.

Scott-12: I don't know what will happen to us if we don't.

Todd-12: You feel you're at the end of your rope.

Scott-13: I thought that time would heal the hurt, but it really hasn't. I didn't realize it, but up 'til the accident life had been pretty easy for us. This was such a shock it threw us for a loss. We weren't prepared, I guess. Maybe people never are.

Todd-13: Ummmmmmmmmmm.

Scott-14: At first we couldn't even talk about it. But just recently we began to think about it and discuss it together, something we haven't done for too many years. Perhaps, if we keep it up, we'll finally be able to understand it, work something out.

Todd-14: You feel there's some hope now that you're working on it together.

Scott-15: Yes, I think so . . . I hope so. (She glanced at the clock on the desk.) My goodness! It's already 9:30 and I've taken the whole evening with our problems. Did you have something you wanted to tell us about?

Todd-15: No, I really wanted to get acquainted with you and your family and to say we're glad Ricky is in the nursery department. I brought his book for the fall quarter. It is for Ricky to keep. I'll leave it, and we can discuss it later. . . . I'll be back in this neighborhood making calls next week. Would you like me to drop by?

Scott-16: No, that won't be necessary . . . but it has been good to talk with you. *Could* you drop in? I'd love to see you, and I'll have some coffee for us. I really do want to talk about the church.

Todd-16: Let's do that then. I'll be here Wednesday about 3:30. Goodnight, Mrs. Scott.

Scott-17: Goodnight, Mrs. Todd, and thank you so much.

There is a listening skill that every person who plans to visit in the home should master. This skill is not a bag of tricks, nor is it beyond the ability of most people. What is required is to listen with ears and mind and heart. To put it another way, it means listening for the *words and ideas* being expressed, for the *meaning* behind the words, and for the feelings that lie underneath it all. In the usual conversation we respond to words and ideas, occasionally to meanings, rarely to feelings. Most of us are unaware that all conversation springs from feelings, which are as real a part of the communication as are the words used. Skill in understanding the feelings being expressed and in responding then to both the words and the feelings of the parent is the way that the visitor's listening really is a help. To have one's problems, fears, guilt, and whatever else, sincerely understood and accepted by another without shock or judgment is like opening the floodgates before turbulent waters. The angry, churning waters suddenly find release; the churning slows down, the currents begin to find their rightful place and direction, the flood becomes dissipated. To listen to and understand another in this way provides him some release from his tensions, some clarification of the elements of his conflict, and eventually some understanding and insight that enables him to deal more satisfactorily with his problem.

The listener-visitor does not hand out these insights to the parent. What does he do? How does one listen and respond to another with understanding?

1. The listener *clarifies*. He restates simply and clearly, in neutral fashion, the ideas and feelings that the parent may have expressed in a long and emotionally involved way. Mrs. Todd's fifth response illustrates this.

2. The listener *accepts*. The words and feelings expressed in Mrs. Scott-6 and -10 are hostile, directed toward the church and God, and flung at Mrs. Todd who, in a sense, represented both at that moment. Mrs. Todd did not feel attacked, neither for herself, nor God, nor the church; she made no remark in defense. She understood and accepted Mrs. Scott's feelings: "After your experiences you've come to wonder if the church isn't a lot of nice words that don't mean anything." This is also illustrated in Todd-7.

3. The listener *becomes a mirror* for the other person. By his responses he tries to hold up before the other the ideas and meanings and feelings that are all a part of the problem, so that the other can see them clearly and choose for himself which ones he wants to work on first. For example, Mrs. Todd-3 reflected the *idea* that having to move away from their minister made the problem much worse. Scott-4 decided No. Later, Mrs. Todd-8 reflected the feelings and meaning expressed in Scott-8, and Mrs. Scott continued her story.

What the visitor *does not do* in a counseling conversation with parents is equally as important as what she does do. What she does not say, the kinds of responses she does not make, should be studied carefully in the preparation the visitor makes before undertaking her job.

95

1. The visitor does *not divert* the conversation. A parent under such great stress that he has decided to tell you his story will tell it, in whatever order and with whatever understanding he has of it or cares to share with you. *Almost every question is a diversion*, a distraction to the parent. Mrs. Todd might well have asked a question at almost any pause in Mrs. Scott's story. It would have been a natural thing to do because the story was slow in being told. But Mrs. Scott's feelings of desperation, of vexation with her husband because of the demands of his job, of doubts about the help their last church offered them, and of the sincerity of any church, were an important part of Mrs. Scott's turmoil. These feelings were on top, in the front line of the battle, and had to be dealt with before Mrs. Scott could look behind them to see what had produced them.

Suppose the visitor had asked one or two questions that would help her make sense of this rather disjointed story; such as " What did Mr. Gray do or say that was such a help to you? " This is an interruption. Mrs. Scott had not planned to relate this; it was not significant to her as she saw her problem. Nonetheless, out of courtesy, she would probably have answered it, and had the listener-visitor accepted the answer without further question, Mrs. Scott would very likely have resumed her story at whatever point was important for her to relate. However, if the listener-visitor had asked another question, and then just one more, Mrs. Scott would probably have withdrawn from the relationship. It might even have seemed to the unknowing listener that her tensions were subsiding. That would not have been the case; they would only have been clamped in more tightly. For Mrs. Scott would be feeling, " I have made a mistake. You don't really want to hear my story as I see it and feel it. You want to hear it in your order and just the parts of it you think are important. I guess you can't really help me after all." From that point on the counseling conversation would be of little or no help to Mrs. Scott, and the relationship between the two women would likely be no more than superficial friendship.

Other diversionary remarks are the ones that intend to support, to offer encouragement, such as: " Tell me all about it," or " You can confide in me just how you think and feel." This is almost a too-eager response. It might make the parent feel, " I wonder if I can trust this person.. What will she do with all this stuff I'm going to tell her? " or " What relief! At last I've found someone who'll know what I should do if I just tell her the whole story." Undoubtedly, the visitor would not intend either of her remarks to result in either of these feelings, but the possibility of this occurring would be very real.

2. The visitor does not generalize. " I know another family with the same problem," or " Such things as death come to everyone," makes the parent feel on the one hand that the listener-visitor does not know what her problem is because no one else could have the same problem or, on the other hand, that the visitor does not care about the specific problems and difficulties arising from Ronnie's death. The second remark is almost a rejection. " It happens to everyone; you have to figure it out yourself."

3. The visitor does not analyze or probe: " Was Ricky very dependent upon Ronnie? "

> . . . or interpret: " You're blaming the church for not giving you a faith."

> . . . or solve: " What you should do is . . ."

For the listener to make any of these responses is to imply to the parent that she, the visitor, will be able to advise or suggest an answer or a way to handle the problem. As a matter of fact, very rarely can anyone do this for another, and in this kind of relationship such a course of action is completely out of key.

4. She does not moralize or sentimentalize: " Your faith will see you through this sorrow."

> . . . or judge: " You should have come to us at the church as soon as you moved here, and not waited so long."

The place for sermons to be spoken is from the pulpit; not from one person to another in a face-to-face relationship that depends upon mutual respect and understanding.

5. She does not agree or disagree. She keeps her own feelings,

97

judgments, and ideas out of the situation. She does not take sides, or commit herself to a point of view. If the parent asks her point-blank to do this, she replies in all honesty, " I don't know what to think, Mrs. Blank " or " I don't know who is right, Mrs. Jones. I'm afraid I don't know enough about the situation to have good judgment. Perhaps as we think through it some more, you'll begin to see yourself what the right answer is." Or, she responds by clarifying the meaning and the feeling behind the question as in Todd-11.

It should be said that this analysis of the " do's " and " don'ts " of a counseling conversation is not a list of specific unalterable rules. Here are guide lines culled from many people's experiences. If the listener understands them and observes them, the parent will be able to express his thoughts more freely and explore his feelings more deeply than he otherwise might.

But equally important is it that you, the nursery visitor, be yourself. Trust your own instincts, do not deny your own humanness. You can learn how to participate in this kind of creative dialogue without canceling out your own personality. Having acquired some skills and understandings of teaching has made you no less yourself. So learning some methods of creative conversation will enhance your ability to become a helpful and understanding friend. This is not a stilted, artificial, unfeeling relationship. In fact, it is exactly the opposite of that.

If a nursery home visitor can, and will, prepare herself with the skills and understandings that will enable her to engage in this kind of creative counseling conversation, she will have learned one more way to extend Christian love and concern to others. The relationship here described is essentially one of person to person, an " I " to a " Thou." Such a relationship as here described shows clearly what the person visiting in the name of the church believes about persons: that each person is unique, his problems and concerns are unique; that the way he sees and feels about his situation is truth for him; that he has within himself the capacity to handle his own situation, to solve his own problems, to grow in self-understanding; that his need is for the kind of help that frees him to do these things without another's taking from him the responsibility for his life.

The home visitor makes her role quite clear in these respects by this very method of listening and responding. She says, in effect, that she will stand by, but that she cannot assume responsibility for Mrs. Scott's life. This is a relief to Mrs. Scott who really wants to handle her life herself, as mixed up as it is. So does every person. " I want to do it mySELF! " And throughout the conversation the visitor tries constantly to put herself in the other's place, to see the world as the other person sees it, to participate in the other person's hurts and joys as though she were standing right there within the other's skin. There are two biblical injunctions that describe this personal relationship of Christian love: " Bear one another's burdens " — the visitor extends her love and understanding to the one who is troubled; and ". . . each man will have to bear his own load " — the visitor helps the parent carry his own responsibility.

FOR YOU TO THINK ABOUT

1. How can a visit to the home of an aggressive, disturbing child in the nursery group be of help to the teacher of the group? to the child? to the parents?

2. In a home visit that centers around a discussion of the child, what kinds of things about the child will you report to the parents? What kinds of things will you try to learn from them?

3. Practice responding to a creative counseling conversation by having someone read Mrs. Scott's remarks to you and write down what you consider a good response. Check it against the record and against the " do's " and " don'ts."

4. Contrive a counseling conversation between a parent and a teacher and use it as a basis for a training session with teachers and nursery visitors prior to making calls.

5. Suppose you feel at the close of a visit with the parents of one of your nursery children that they need better-qualified and more skilled help than you have given them or can give them. What should you say? What should you do?

CHAPTER SEVEN

Role Playing: A Technique for Learning How to Make a Home Visit

ONE WAY to play a game better is to practice it. Often we feel that if we only could have practiced our part in some human relationship situation before we had to act in it, we would have behaved much differently and have felt much better about how we had acquitted ourselves. It is possible to do just this. The technique, or method for doing it, is called role playing.

Role playing is a method for learning about the dynamics of human relationships; that is, how what I do and say affects me and the people about me. It is also possible to understand from a role-playing situation some of the factors, the feelings, the reasons that *lie behind* what all of the persons involved do and say. Role playing is a technique by which teachers, or anyone, can grow in self-understanding and in the understanding of other people. Role playing can provide for teachers a practice situation in which they can learn how to make a call, what to say, how to respond; and then together evaluate how helpful the call has been for the family.

Teachers of the nursery department might well spend an evening practicing, through role playing, how to make calls in the homes of their children. Then, after a few weeks in which each teacher has made four to six home calls, the teachers could well spend another evening together role playing the situations that puzzled them, creating fictional situations to resemble the ones in which they felt they should have behaved differently, and analyzing the situations to see what the trouble was.

There are four steps in using role playing as a learning situation:

1. Create a situation
2. Characterize the people in it
3. Play it
4. Analyze it

This whole process will move much faster, with greater learning for the teachers, if the number of teachers working together is no more than ten. Large groups tend to produce spectators instead of creators who are personally involved in the learning. And role playing is most effective without spectators. It is not entertainment, although it might well prove entertaining. Its primary function is to demonstrate some principles in human relationships. All the people working at the role playing are learners; some are volunteers who do some of the playing of the roles.

Create the Situation

This is the product of group thinking in which the teachers together create a family, give the members ages and names, locate the home at some specific place in the community, describe the family's church relationship, and imagine the preparatory conversations that have taken place and the plans which the teacher has made for this particular home visit.

Characterize the People

Here the teachers determine what all the people in the situation are like: how each one feels about himself as teacher or parent or child; his status in the community, at church, on his job; the goals he strives for, the convictions he holds, his insecurities. It is not necessary to make a description of each person in each of these categories, but there must be enough of a real person created so that the person playing the role will be able to speak and act as this person. This is different from describing the person by a set of adjectives or phrases.

For example, if the role player is told that the teacher he is to play does not really enjoy teaching, yet feels obligated to take her turn; tolerates the immaturity of children, and is in no wise delighted with it or fascinated by their growth; and is fearful lest she may be tripped up by what she does not know about God and Jesus and the Bible; then he has a whole set of meanings and attitudes from which to speak and act. But if the teacher whom he will play is described in some such way as, "she is lazy, not interested in learning, does the same thing with the children Sunday after Sunday," he then has only a superficial understanding of that teacher.

In a role-playing situation in which the teachers are practicing making home visits, the demonstration is easier to play and to learn from if there are no more than three people in the situation — the teacher and the two parents. In fact, at the beginning, it would be even better to have just two — the teacher and one parent. The more people involved, the more complicated the conversation becomes, the harder the situation is to follow and to remember. Children might well be present when a teacher is actually making a home visit, but, for learning how, take simple situations first and look at one thing at a time. Eventually teachers, who are learning how to make home visits, will want to try out one or more situations with children. This practice will help the teachers discover what they should do and say to the child who is in the nursery group as well as to any older brothers and sisters who may be present during a home visit.

A word from the experience of other teachers' and parents' groups, which have included children in their role-playing situations, might be of help here. Unless the adult playing the role of the child is both a skilled role player and very sensitive to and understanding of the world as the child sees it, the characterization of the child is likely not to come off. The part is "hammed" and the role players dissolve in laughter. This is not to say that playing a child cannot be done. It can, but it is difficult to do well, and the younger the child involved the more difficult it is.

Two other rules it is always wise to observe are: do not play real people known to anyone in the group (this also means no one should play himself), and do not play real situations known to or related by anyone in the group. There are two reasons for this. First, the degree of involvement in the learning process is greater if the group creates and sets up its own role-playing situation. Second, no one can ever really live the life of another. He brings to it his own past experiences and interpretations, and these keep coming through the conversation in such a way that the role playing is not true to the " real " person who is being played. Besides, it does not take much imagination to foresee that there could easily develop antagonism, defensiveness, and little anxieties among those involved in such a situation instead of the free atmosphere of learning that the method tries to create.

Play the Situation

The situation is created, the scene is set, the characters are described. Now find the teachers who will assume the roles. This done, the total group of teachers might well review together the kind of person each character is and then allow each player a few moments to think himself into the role. The players are not told what to say nor what ideas they hold. These develop from the personality the group has given each role as the player understands it. *This means that in the playing there is no right way or wrong way to act.* Role playing is a dynamic situation. No one knows what will happen before it is over, just as in a real life situation. What does happen grows out of the words and feelings and interpretations of the participants.

It is helpful if each teacher who is observing the role playing assumes for himself one of the roles being played. That is, he thinks the responses and feels the feelings of one of the persons the group has just created. Doing this makes each teacher less a spectator and more a participator in the learning experience. Each person present should have a paper and pencil, so he can record his thoughts and feelings as he experiences them, and so he can write down exact words or phrases that might be studied in the analysis.

The role playing will be better done and what happens in it better understood if the people observing it maintain silence.

The role playing lasts as long as the players themselves determine. Either they end the situation with good-bys, or the players run out of ideas for continuing, or something funny strikes someone and the situation ends. It does not matter how or when it ends so long as the interchange has gone on long enough for some personal relationships to develop. However, the situation should not continue so long that those who are watching lose interest or find themselves with more material than they can remember and profitably discuss.

Analyze the Situation

In the analysis the teachers continue as they have proceeded so far: sharing questions, insights, and ideas. Each does her own learning on the basis of what she herself has discovered. Some questions to consider in discussing the role playing are listed below. The teachers themselves will think of others.

1. What was happening here (that is, in the situation played)?

2. How did each character feel about herself after this was over? (That is, how did the parent, Mrs. Brown, and the nursery visitor, Miss Jones, feel?) First, each teacher, if the group numbers no more than ten, could share her personal reaction as she identified herself with one of the characters. Then see how the players themselves felt, *as the persons in the role.*

3. Did anyone understand the feelings of anyone else, as well as the words, or try to?

4. What kind of call did this turn out to be? How did the parents use the time, or didn't they have a chance to use it? How do you think this call affects their feeling about the church and about the church school for their child?

5. What did the teacher-visitor learn about this family that would be helpful for her teaching; for her relationship to the nursery child?

6. What would you predict the future relationship of this family and the teacher to be?

The teachers who watched the role-playing situation might each have said or done something different from what the role player did, but that fact does not say that one was right and the other was wrong. It may be that during the period spent in analyzing the role playing, the teachers will decide that some responses are better than others — that is the purpose for doing the role playing; but this should in no way be understood as a judgment upon the " rightness " or skill of the persons playing the roles. Whatever is said or done is " right " for the situation and can be instructive.

Role playing as a method of learning is fun and it is exciting. It is true to our belief in persons as creative spirits, each with his own needs and his own talents, which he will use if he is free to or will bury if he feels inadequate. Learning by living through a fictional experience, such as role playing, frees each person to take a chance, to become involved, to risk himself, because what happens does not really count. No one can lose status or prestige because the situation is not real. Because no one is in error and no one is sitting in judgment, the climate is as free as possible from such anxieties as: " I wonder how I'm doing? " " I wonder what that other teacher thinks of me? " " Did I make the right response? "

Try it! It is fun! And it can be adapted to countless situations as a method for learning.

The Teachers Spend an Evening Role Playing in Preparation for Making Home Visits

Alice Todd, Jane, Harriet, and Ellen had planned to visit the home of each nursery child during the month of November. At their regular meeting early in October they worked out the specific details concerning who would call on which family, how to make appointments beforehand, their " reason " for making the call, how long to stay, and so on. Although the quarter would be well under way, they decided that for their program it would not be too late to take to each home the curriculum material planned for the child. They listed some of the important points about the book and about the activities in the Sunday three-year-old group which they hoped to discuss with the parents. Then they decided to try out their skill as home callers. Jane wanted to be the teacher in the scene and she named herself Mrs. Jackson. Harriet volunteered to be the parent, Mrs. Motherchild.

The teachers characterized Mrs. Jackson as the mother of three children, all older than nursery age; a rather new member of the community and a quite recent member of the church. She has a background of church activity, but this is her first year of teaching three-year-olds. She feels strongly that the young child's home is more important in his life than she and the church are, and she is very pleased to find that the philosophy and the teaching materials of the church support this point of view. During this visit she wants to get this across to Mrs. Motherchild, as well as to know her better.

Mrs. Motherchild, the teachers decided, was new to the church, too, having come about three years before from another denomination in another city. The family has two children in the grades of the church school; and Dickie, their youngest, is in the three-year-old group. Mr. Motherchild is an inactive church member, not hostile to the church, but not convinced that it does or thinks or stands for anything very important.

The role playing began. After a few moments spent in greeting each other and in some light talk about the weather, Mrs. Motherchild — to Mrs. Jackson's surprise — came right to the point.

Mrs. Motherchild: I've been wanting to talk with one of you teachers in the nursery for some weeks now. Tell me about your program there. What do you do with the children?

Mrs. Jackson: I'm glad you want to know, because that is what I came to talk with you about. (Teacher and mother then spent five minutes together looking through Dickie's book. Mrs. Jackson explained; Mrs. Motherchild listened, asked a few questions.)

Mrs. M: The children really don't do anything but play, then, do they?

Mrs. J: Well, you might say that. I'm sure it must seem that way to anyone looking in the room.

Mrs. M: I don't know what else could be going on. You said you don't sit them down to teach them anything, you don't even read all of them the story from their book every Sunday, so there's no way to learn anything except maybe how to put a new puzzle together.

Mrs. J: We believe that the kind of learning that is making Dickie a good person can't be done in one hour on Sunday mornings, or two hours, either, if he's there for the extended session. It's a job that goes on all the time, and you and his home are more important at this point than the church is.

Mrs. M: What good is the church for Dickie, then? I might as well not make the effort to get him there, as my husband was just telling me last Sunday morning when we were going through our usual struggle.

Mrs. J: We try at church to provide a good experience for Dickie with children his own age and with teachers who care for him. We try to help him when he needs help, always to understand him. My job is to tie shoes or blow noses, steady a block tower, or arrange for a turn on one of the horses, carry on a conversation about diesel trucks with one "big boy," and talk with another child who has a new baby sister at home. We teach by responding to the needs of the children as we understand them, and it's great fun to do when you don't also have to answer the phone, watch the soup, and hang up the wash. If Dickie enjoys coming, then he must have a good feeling toward the church, and we've made a good beginning.

Mrs. M: He enjoys it, I can't deny that. Whenever we drive past it he points it out with pride, "That's our church where we go on Sundays." But I don't see what other thing you do that I don't do. I do all those things, too, when I can. Whose job is it to teach him about Jesus and prayer?

This role-playing situation lasted for nearly ten minutes and the teachers discussed it for more than an hour. They took up, in turn, the questions suggested under "Analysis of Role Playing" in this chapter, and then finally came back to the question that was always lurking in the corners and sometimes came right out in the open at every teachers' meeting the rest of the year: What does it mean to teach a three-year-old in the church?

Earlier, the leaders had learned they had to answer that question in order to develop some competence and convictions about the job they had undertaken. Now they found they had to answer the same question in order to be of significant help to the parents of the three-year-olds.

FOR YOU TO THINK ABOUT

1. Assume the role of Dickie's teacher, Mrs. Jackson, and write out your own answer to Mrs. Motherchild's final question. Then read the answer as though you were Mrs. Motherchild and imagine how you would feel about Mrs. Jackson and the church.

2. At a teachers' meeting, use this characterization of Mrs. Jackson and Mrs. Motherchild to set up your first role-playing situation, but let each role player create his own dialogue out of his own interpretation of the character he represents. Remember, there is no right and no wrong response in role playing.

3. In the role-playing excerpt in this chapter how do you think Mrs. Jackson was feeling about herself as a nursery home visitor? Why?

4. What needs to happen in the relationship between Mrs. Jackson and Mrs. Motherchild in order to call the home visit a " successful " one?

5. Try a role-playing situation in which you, the teacher, call on a friend, a neighbor, or another church member to invite her to teach with you in the three-year-old room. Role play, too, the phone conversation preceding the call. If you have no one to carry on this dialogue with you (a husband or wife will do), write it out. It is not so spontaneous, but you will find it instructive.

PART FOUR

Meetings With the Parents

Let love be genuine; hate what is evil, hold fast to what is good; love one another with brotherly affection; outdo one another in showing honor. Never flag in zeal, be aglow with the Spirit, serve the Lord. Rejoice in your hope, be patient in tribulation, be constant in prayer.

Romans 12: 9-12

CHAPTER EIGHT

Fun Meetings, Work Meetings, and Information Meetings

RECOGNIZING that the child's home is the most influential determinant of his religious growth, an increasing number of churches are spending much time and effort in various kinds of church-home programs. One of the most significant of these programs involves working with groups of parents.

There certainly is no one way to work with parents; but there are some ways that are more rewarding to parents than are others. Regular, individual, personal contact between church and parents, as in the home visit, becomes for the parents, and therefore, for the families, a help in working through the little, vexing, day-by-day problems, as well as a strong support in times of great crisis or trouble, if the home visitor has the skills and understanding required to do this. When a good relationship already exists between home and church, the family will know where to turn when it needs help.

There also can be great good in meeting with groups of parents. Churches have done many different things in parents' meetings, but the purpose behind all of them is pretty much the same; to get parents interested in the church's religious education program and to enlist their co-operation in it; to help parents find guidance and support for their job of Christian nurture in the home; to acquaint parents with other parents of the same age children in order to build within the church community a core of people who share a common concern and conviction; to help parents grow as mature Christian persons.

Whatever the purpose or the program, church and home alike lose a great deal if the parents' meetings become in fact a mothers' club. A family is a group of people who cannot escape each other, because they live together. They must constantly take each other into account, even absent members, and communicate with each other. The love quality of their relationship, the sensitivity, the thoughtfulness, the concern of each for each may be pretty shallow, but nonetheless, every member is part of this relationship.

Each person contributes to the kind of life the family enjoys or endures together. A mother alone may be able to do a great deal to improve the quality of the family's life. A mother and father working together can change completely the family's attitudes and outlook, the way its members get along with one another, the family's standard of values — what is important to its life, the family dreams and, in fact, the family destiny. These kinds of changes can hardly take place unless both the powerful people in the family, the parents, work at them together.

Many of the families in our democracy are still patriarchies in that it is the father who sets the " tone " in such matters as attitudes toward others; what is worth giving your life for (If you want to be a success . . .); how to get along in the world (Life's a struggle; you've got to get what you've got coming when you can get it, and let each man look out for himself); and so forth. In some families it is accepted that fathers know best. The reason they do, the argument runs, is that they are out in the world every day, in the struggle and the competition that is part of making a living. Mothers live within the peace of four walls where " you can be honest and loving and forgiving without losing everything you've been working for." Yes, churches do need to work with mothers and fathers.

Who plans the meetings? The leadership of the church minister, director of Christian education, church school superintendent, nursery teacher, chairman of the board of Christian education) working with a group of four or five parents, men and women, is probably the best committee. The parents, in this case, are not couples, because the more families represented in the thinking, the better the meetings are likely to be.

There are at least four kinds of parents' meetings that can be considered:

1. Meetings that are mainly fun, such as " get acquainted " teas and morning coffee hours for mothers, potluck suppers and family festivals for the entire family.

2. Meetings for the purpose of repairing and rejuvenating the equipment of the nursery department.

3. Meetings that are informative; that is, they intend to help parents better understand themselves, their children, and their church. The programs vary, for example:

   a. A film — on child development or the nursery program of the church
   b. A talk, or a panel discussion
   c. A presentation by a teacher, the minister, the director of religious education, or other leader, of the curriculum material used in the nursery program.

4. Meetings to help parents grow toward Christian maturity. These meetings seek to provide for parents an *experience together* through which they can grow in their understanding of the Christian life and in their ability to live it in their homes. The meetings are not designed primarily to provide parents with answers to their own or to their children's questions about God, Jesus, the Bible, and so forth, although such questions may be dealt with during the meeting. A fuller description of the nature and purpose of this type of meeting is given in chapter nine.

It is probable that each of these types of meetings will also have within it some aspects of one or more of the other types.

For example, an evening spent rejuvenating equipment might well be informative on such a matter as the wise choice of toys All of these types of meetings should provide something of the experience of fun for the sake of the morale of the group. There must be some sense of personal involvement, of "This is me, functioning," for each parent present, if there is to develop any group spirit and any individual sense of belonging and enjoyment. Passive participation — if there can be such a thing — such as listening or watching is usually not called fun unless the spectator has a strong sense of identification with what is going on, as at a baseball game.

There is good reason for each of these kinds of meetings. A total year's program for parents and for families might well include all four types. Each church must decide for itself which kinds of meetings, how many, how frequently, and so forth, are required for the job it needs to get done. There is one rule that applies to all these meetings, all the time: DO THEM WELL!

People become impatient with slow starts, ambling or poorly planned programs, and endings that occur because it is late rather than because the task set before the group is accomplished. No one, mothers or fathers, has much enthusiasm to become part of a parents' program that is dull and ineffective.

Instead:

a. *Have everything needed ready before the meeting starts:* paper and pencils, blackboard and eraser, film projector and screen set up and tried out, chairs arranged, table in place, refreshments — if there are to be some — ready to serve, responsibilities assigned, and leaders on hand, on time. The leader of the meeting, or the hostess, or some designated person should be on hand fifteen to twenty minutes ahead of time. Early comers should not have to find the key to the church and turn on the lights, unless they are designated to do this.

b. *Have a time schedule worked out and stick to it.* Begin on time, end on time. If some part of the program, for example, a parents' panel, runs on and on so that there will be no time for discussion, the leader of the meeting will have to terminate the panel or eliminate part of the discussion period. When such a thing happens, it may be because members have not made adequate preparation beforehand.

c. *If practicable, include only the parents of children in one class or department.* This, of course, depends upon the type of meeting being held and the size of the class, department, or church school. Usually a group of eighteen to twenty people is freer to engage in discussion; able to know each other better; and, if the group members are parents of one class of children, able to find their common concerns more quickly than a larger group can.

d. *Think through at the close of the planning session and before the meeting: What is our goal for this meeting and will the program we have planned achieve it?* Often a meeting is planned around a film, or a talk, or a panel discussion, and followed with refreshments in the hope that the parents who attend will go home feeling, "That's a swell group of people. I'm glad we're part of such a group. Wonder when the next meeting will be?" Such high group morale and feeling of belonging does not usually result from an information meeting followed by fifteen minutes of polite and trivial conversation over coffee and doughnuts.

Meetings That Are Fun

If the goal for the meeting is to begin the formation of a parents' group that will develop purposes and goals and patterns of behaving all its own, certainly the parents must have some opportunities to get to know each other, and planned fun is often a good beginning. Here are some suggestions:

1. Begin the evening with a potluck supper, or end it with refreshments. Eating together provides an opportunity for people to talk informally without self-consciousness.

2. The first activities or games should involve each person present in some kind of total group effort requiring no great amount of previous skill or experience. No one should "stick out" because he cannot participate in what is planned, or because the game requires an "It."

The simple singing folk games, such as "Ach Ja!", are usuall quite successful here. The steps and movements are easy to learn they are not physically arduous; and the progression of them lead to changes in partners. Many of the simple ones are on records Others can be found in books of games. All that is required is room that is large enough, a good piano player or a record player and a leader who knows the steps and the words. Sometimes group of parents who have spent an evening ahead of time learn ing two or three singing games can become the leaders and the demonstrators at the meeting for the total group.

Very little is gained in trying to build a group by such activities as "brain teasers" and "ice breakers." These are usually indi vidual activities that the group members do at the same time but there is no person-to-person interchange of dramatic social quality. They involve playing with words or names, which can be pleasant enough, but this activity usually remains on a very superficial level of communication.

Following singing games there can be some team games, such as relays, blowing a ping pong ball across the table, or a Bible treasure hunt.

3. Try some creative activities, something where the parents own ideas become part of the fun. This probably is most easily done by small groups where no one person's status in the group is at stake, but each group, as a small unit, produces something to be shared with all the others. Dramatic episodes, skits, and panto mimes, using only the props the environment provides, are often fun. Each group might prepare a two- or three-minute scene on a subject such as, "One good way a family can have fun together" or they might do some charades.

4. End the evening with worship — good worship, not trite not stilted, nor the kind that usually comes to mind with the announcement that, "So and so will lead us in some brief devo tions." Do not let the period of worship be the least meaningful part of the evening. Some one has to work at this. Perhaps the minister can do it, perhaps a few parents working with him can do it even better. Again include an opportunity for personal

116

involvement, in addition to singing a hymn together. Try a litany or a choral reading, written particularly for this evening, lifting up in praise and thankfulness such things as the human love that exists in families, the interdependence of men, the church that keeps before its people a picture of the life that is good to live, and so forth. The words and phrases of this litany or choral reading should say specific things, not vague generalizations about the bounty of the earth and the graciousness of God. Ears are dulled with too much listening to such familiar phraseology.

5. If there are refreshments, let them end the evening.

If this meeting has been well done, each parent will go home with the feeling that, " I was there." This means the " I " which is more than the body. It includes " my mind, my spirit, my Self. I gave myself to others in fun and enthusiasm; I revealed something of myself. And the other people there did the same thing for me. I now know something about them, what they are like, and they know something about me."

After such a meeting parents may be overheard saying such things as, " Don and Jean Roberts seem to be a swell couple; we ought to get to know them better," or, " I found out that Bob Jones works in an office only two blocks from mine," or, " Sarah Bonn asked me to go to Mothers' Club with her next Monday night, and I'm so glad because I've been wanting to go." These are the personal relationships that become the foundation of the fellowship of the church.

Work Meetings — To Improve Rooms and Equipment

Parents can have great fun and the three-year-old room in the church can become a lovely place if the parents spend a few evenings with hammers, saws, paint, needles and thread, soap and water, renovating and cleaning the room and the equipment. The most important factor to a successful work night is the *preparation beforehand*. This takes considerable planning and setting up of the room and materials to be used for the work. But unless it is done well, the parents feel as though their time has been ill-used, which it has.

1. Divide the work to be done into small enough units so that one evening's work will complete it. If there is work remaining, start it another evening. Don't start everything at one time and get all of it *half* finished. It makes the job seem colossal if nothing gets finished in one night, and picking up where the group left off is difficult.

2. Find a parent to take charge of each work unit; for example, toy repair, toy painting, furniture painting, shelf and cupboard cleaning or painting, new construction, doll clothes repair, and so forth. Each of these parents may find one or perhaps two others to work with him or her in gathering ahead of time the equipment and materials needed and in laying out the work for a designated number of people.

3. Have something for *everyone* to do and have it ready. Let there be no standing around, no waiting for something to happen, or for someone to come with the materials or equipment.

4. Refreshments at the end of the meeting will bring the whole group together in a feeling of fellowship and accomplishment.

Meetings for Learning

Often parents just don't know: what to expect of a child the age of theirs; what the religious education program and philosophy of the church is for their child; how to use discipline, and countless other things. Some of these things the church does know about and can tell the parents. The subjects that can be included in meetings for learning and the methods that can be used are numerous. Common forms of programs are using audiovisual materials (film, filmstrip, recording, or slides); having a talk by an expert or an authority; having a panel discussion; planning a presentation of the curriculum of the church school by the minister, director of Christian education, superintendent, or teacher of the class or department.

In addition to the general suggestions that apply to all meetings, there are some specific " do's " and " don'ts " for this type of meeting.

A. If the content of the meeting is presented by a film, film-strip, recording, or slides, the person who will conduct the meeting must preview the material at least once, perhaps more than that. If the facts presented by the film (or filmstrip, recording, or slides) are important enough that parents should discuss them and understand them, the leader of the meeting must know what the facts are, how they are presented, and what they ought to mean to the parents.

Having previewed the film, the leader of the meeting must then work out on paper the points that should be discussed by the group as preparation for viewing the film, and the points that should be raised for discussion following the film. Preparation of the group beforehand and discussion immediately afterward are good and necessary teaching techniques for the use of all audio-visual materials.

Let us suppose that the visual material being used is a sound filmstrip, setting forth the nature of the nursery program for children in the church school.

1. Introduce the visual material, tell who made it, why it was made (its purpose), what use we are going to make of it tonight.

2. For the discussion, the group should be sitting in a circle of chairs, the leader sitting in the circle, too. The leader might say something such as, " Before we look at this filmstrip, let's spend a few minutes thinking about our nursery children in our church. Why are you bringing your children to the nursery department? What can they get out of it? What good will it do them? " Let the group think and talk about these questions for about ten minutes. Then the leader, or a designated group member, should summarize the points made and list them on a chalkboard in the front of the room to one side of the screen where everyone can see the list.

3. Move the chairs, if necessary, so that all can see the screen, and show the filmstrip.

4. Re-form the circle, the leader sitting down with the other members of the group. For group discussion and good group

feeling, it is important that everyone be able to see who is talking and that no one has a "cold seat," geographically outside the group, from where he does not have to participate. The leader says, "Now that we've done some thinking of our own and have seen and heard some ideas in the filmstrip, what comments do you have to make?"

When these topmost feelings and ideas are expressed, the group members might then discuss at a more thoughtful and contemplative level such questions as: What were the children learning in the nursery program in the filmstrip? How does this learning contribute to their religious growth? What should we be doing to improve the experience our children are having? What part do parents play in the Christian education of their children?

The leader should not have these questions written on a little slip of paper which he or she reads off to the group, waiting for the answers, and going on to the next question. This is poor teaching. Rather, having previewed the visual material and carefully worked out a plan ahead of time, the leader has the points to be included in his or her mind and can introduce them into the group discussion wherever they logically fit. The group itself will undoubtedly take up some of the points without the leader's questions having to be asked.

There are other ways a group can be prepared to view visual material. The method devised depends largely on what is in the material, what the leader decides should be particularly emphasized and understood, and how his own imagination works in thinking through a "lesson plan" for the parents' meeting. The important thing is that there be adequate thoughtful preparation which will stimulate interest in the visual material and give each parent something specific for which to look.

Likewise, the form of the discussion following the viewing does not matter. What matters is that each person has a chance to express, either to a small group or the total group, his reaction to the material. Following this, each person or the group must have time to consider how and in what ways the ideas of the visual material have personal meaning for him.

B. If the program of the meeting is to be a talk by an " expert " or a presentation by a panel of parents:

1. Be sure your speaker, or the panel, has a clear understanding of what he is to speak on; some background information about his audience; some idea of the church's intentions with this group of parents; how long he is to talk and what will happen after he is finished; and whether he has any further responsibilities following his presentation. Give him a subject. No one enjoys talking to a group on, " Whatever you know that you think would be good for us."

2. Following the talk or the panel discussion, try using *buzz groups* to allow each person to have a chance to discuss his ideas, state his reactions, become involved personally. To do this, before the meeting begins, have the chairs arranged in small circles of no more than eight chairs in each circle. As the chairs are occupied, the groups are formed. Groups of fewer than five should combine or join other groups. If such an arrangement is not possible, the leader of the meeting, at the close of the talk, asks the parents to form themselves into small groups of not more than eight people. He or she must wait a few minutes until this is done, and then say, " We shall now have ten or fifteen minutes to share our reactions to what our speaker has said to us tonight, and to formulate questions that we would like to have him discuss for us before he leaves." Or the leader might feel that to give the buzz groups some direction for their " buzzing," they should have a specific question put to them, growing out of the material presented. Each group might then report, through a designated group member, the group's thinking to the total group. Often the leader summarizes each report in a few words and writes it on a chalkboard, so that the variety of thinking as well as the frequency of agreement is available for all to see when the reporting is completed.

C. If the purpose of the meeting is to acquaint parents with the curriculum material being used in the nursery department and to give them some understanding of the purpose and philosophy underlying it:

1. Put a copy of the material in the hands of the parents, preferably one they can take home.

2. Do some demonstration teaching of a particular Sunday morning program rather than talk in general about a whole quarter's work. By dealing specifically with one Sunday, you will illustrate the philosophy and method of the entire curriculum for that age child.

Set up some of the equipment, use the nursery story, songs, and prayers, just as you would on a Sunday morning, but do not expect the parents to take the part of three-year-olds. They do not do it well, and they feel foolish. Let them listen in and imagine the responses of the children, just as you are doing in the demonstration teaching. Relate as vividly as you can what the activities, the conversation, the social life of the nursery is like on Sunday mornings, citing whatever examples of growth and learning you can relate without betraying a child or embarrassing his parents. You may decide that this latter reporting should be fictional.

3. Plan for the parents to respond through small group discussions or buzz groups. They will be more honest in saying what they think to each other than to the person who presented the material. They might consider, besides sharing their reactions to the material and ideas presented, such questions as: " How — in what ways — do you, as parents, feel you can help your child as he grows to Christian maturity? " or, " What further help can the church be to you in the religious education of your child and how best can we work at it together? "

It is well to avoid giving a group of parents, or anyone, a subject for discussion that focuses attention on the negative aspects of a subject. Avoid such questions for discussion as, " What is omitted in this program for our nursery children? ", " What are we parents not doing which we should be doing? " or, " For some children this curriculum, well-planned as it is, never comes off. They get nothing out of their church school experience. What can you see are the reasons for this?"

To spend the last half of a meeting discussing such things may arouse antagonisms. Some parents will defend the church, or the leader, or the curriculum with more emotion than intelligent reasoning. Also, the group may well feel threatened, not knowing whether the leader is able sincerely to "take" and respond to such a discussion without feeling attacked himself. And it is likely to be a hindrance to good morale within the parents' group, as well as to create doubts in parents' minds about the worthwhileness of the church school experience and whether the church itself knows what it is trying to do. Avoiding such discussions is not to suggest that the church should not make use of the critical judgments about its life that might well make the church more nearly the body of Christ. It is to say that no one can make intelligent, constructive criticism of an idea, a book, a plan, or a program until he first thoroughly understands it. Forty minutes spent listening and watching a demonstration hardly provides this depth of understanding.

FOR YOU TO THINK ABOUT

1. You, the nursery teacher, feel that some regular meetings of the parents of the nursery children would be very desirable.

    a. How will you choose your committee to plan these meetings?

    b. Considering your own situation, what kinds of meetings do you think would be best? (The committee decides, of course, but you must have some ideas.)

    c. Work out several ways that the parents can be invited. Remember that personal contact is always best.

    d. Write out in detail the preparations necessary for the kind of meeting with which you could begin. Include how you will get your committee together, how the parents will be invited, how the program itself will proceed, the kinds of help to be requested from participating parents.

CHAPTER NINE

Meetings to Help Parents Grow Toward Christian Maturity

THE CHURCH that is trying to help parents become more and more able to live as Christians is attempting the most difficult job of all, and also the most worth-while one. This is not to say that the three forms of parents' meetings discussed in chapter eight should be discontinued; not at all. Rather, it is to say that we should not expect a fun meeting, a work meeting, or an information meeting to provide for the parents who come a vital or very profound experience of love, acceptance, or understanding. This is not the primary purpose of these types of meetings. A very different kind of meeting is necessary for such experiences.

Before we describe this kind of meeting, let us first look into the reasons why a church should undertake a program of this kind for parents. A goal in Christian education from nursery through the adult years is to help people live the way Jesus Christ taught, and the way he lived. This means to extend one's love to all men; to accept people no matter what their present condition is or their past behavior has been; to understand people, how they feel on the inside. This means not to reject them, condemn them, or pass judgment upon them.

These are the ways to describe the relationship which the Christian has with all other people. He acts in these ways because he believes that each man is a child of God, that he is of great worth, that to sin against him is to sin against God himself. Jesus taught these things, and he demonstrated them over and over. This is the life God intends all men to live, Jesus said. Because he demonstrated it so completely himself, men came to feel in the years after his death that, in truth, God himself was in Christ.

The church believes that there is something of the spirit of God in each of us. The church also proclaims that the kind of life Jesus lived ought to become the pattern for our lives today in our homes, at work, in the market place, among all men whatever be their age, color, or condition. To help this kind of living take root and grow in the families of our churches is one of our major tasks.

Fortunately, we do not have to work at this entirely on the basis of our best hunches about it. The fields of education, psychology, sociology, and anthropology have given us great insights into how people grow and learn; how attitudes are developed; the importance of personal, first-hand experience; how a person adopts as his own the habits, patterns, and folkways of the group in which he grows up.

Specifically, we know that parents can grow in their ability to love, accept, understand, and forgive their children (and all other people, of course), if parents can experience love, acceptance, understanding, and forgiveness themselves. The parents' groups, which we are about to describe, set out to provide these experiences in human relationships for each parent in such a way that this quality of living could be understood and practiced.

Also, we know that hostility, insecurity, feelings of inadequacy, fear, and defensiveness in the children of our families and our communities, yes, in our world, too, are handicaps to the growth of Christian maturity. Changing these negative feelings and attitudes within a child is a matter of helping a child gain a completely different interpretation of himself, of other people, of what the world is like. We know that these feelings within children are born out of an adult-child relationship plus early experiences that are to the child harsh, threatening, non-loving.

And we know that if a child is to grow through and change these feelings about himself and the world, he must have parents (or a therapist, or foster parents, or a teacher) who will try to understand the world from his point of view, who will engage with him in the struggle to untangle it, who will love him when he is unlovable, rejoice in him, treasure him, treat him as a person, a child of God.

This kind of growth and change in personality is a constant process that needs continuous help and loving care. It cannot be done effectively by even the most creative, well-planned church school program or by the most faithful family observance of worship at church and at home. This growth is primarily a matter of the child's relationship to his parents. The child feels alone, unacceptable, unloved. He does not trust the world, responds to it with timidity or hostility. The parents become concerned. They may feel guilty about having done something wrong and are anxious to help the child "get straightened out." Their very anxiety makes matters worse.

This feeling of alienation between parent and child, of not understanding each other, or not being able to do anything right in the eyes of the other, is not a rare circumstance. All parents and children experience these breaches in their relationship, and the breaches hurt. Often the hurt is not deep; the next day or even the next hour it is forgotten. Many times, however, the hurt is deep: parent and child really do not understand each other; they have an uneasy sense of estrangement; and they want more than anything else to make things right between them.

". . . the worst hurt any of us can experience is the hurt suffered at the hands of someone we love and from whom we expect love," writes Reuel Howe in *Man's Need and God's Action*. He goes on to say that ". . . the only effective healing for person-hurts is person-healing," and "To whatever degree there is true regard and love for others, person-healing occurs." [1]

Let us consider an actual program for parents that was planned

[1] From *Man's Need and God's Action* by Reuel L. Howe. Copyright, The Seabury Press. Used by permission.

to help parents understand themselves, their relationship between one another and with their children; and to increase their capacity to love, to understand, to accept.

The parents met in small groups, no more than seven couples in a group, in each other's homes once a week for six weeks. Parents joined the group meeting on the night most convenient for them. They all had a nursery age child enrolled in the church's Sunday and weekday nursery program.

In the course of the year, two series of six meetings each were held, one in the fall, the other in the spring.

Each series of six meetings had as its subject some aspect of human relations such as " Communication," " Creative Conflict," " Understanding and Accepting Feelings," " How to Treat People as Persons," " The Nature of Love." The program for the evening followed this plan: presentation of the idea; discussion and questions; analysis by the group of its own functioning. Final anonymous evaluation of the series showed that most of the parents rated this series of meetings as the most helpful experience for family living they had had.

In the fall of the year, before the parents' meetings began, the teacher working with the children and parents in this program held at least two conferences with the parents in their homes. During one of these visits, the approaching series was discussed: its form, its method, its purpose. The teacher said something like this: " The purpose of this program is to help all of us as adults grow more skilled in living, understanding, accepting, forgiving other people, including our children. We (meaning the leadership of the church, those who set up the program) believe that the knowledge and skill required to live with children so that they can grow into confident, creative, capable people is not much different from that required to live harmoniously with anybody. At least the principles are the same. What we're after is to learn and understand the principles that underlie good human relationships."

A small committee of five parents and the teacher worked out the title for the series, the details for the first meeting, and sent out the invitations. The parents replied by stating on which night they could come. The groups were thus set up. Each couple was then sent a list of the members of their group and the notice of where and when the first meeting would be held.

The Presentation

Each meeting began with a presentation designed to provide a common experience for the group to respond to, discuss, or question. Any group needs a point of focus, the more dramatic and provocative the better, in order to help it get its collective thinking going. Role playing some fictional situation in human relationships was the most "alive" and most frequently used way to begin.[1]

Out of their experience the parents made these discoveries of things not to do.

a. They found they could not play the part of a nursery age child well, even though they were his parents;

b. Both the characters and the situation in the role playing should be completely fictional, the product of the group's imagination rather than the experience of any one member;

c. It saved time in setting up the role playing if one or two couples brought ideas for situations that might be role played. The group either chose one of these, or, with this start for its thinking, created its own situation.

Although role playing was the most popular method for beginning the meeting, other types of presentations were also used:

1. A brief, cogent statement of an idea by the leader, followed by buzz groups.[2]

2. A dialogue between the leader and a parent illustrating the subject matter for the evening; for example, " Communication Between People."

[1] For more details on the method of role playing, see chapter seven.

[2] Buzz groups are described in chapter eight under " Meetings for Learning." See page 121.

3. A case study of a child no one knew. Each parent was given a mimeographed copy of the case study.

4. A panel presentation by three parents.

5. Pamphlet material to be read beforehand as common preparation. (This was least successful. Unexpected circumstances inevitably prevented some couples from doing the reading.)

The Discussion

During the discussion period that followed the presentation, the teacher, who was the leader of this group, tried consistently to help the group function as a group. That is, she tried to help the group discover what its questions were, what direction it wanted to go, what plans it had to make in order to continue being productive. This is a different approach from the usual notion of discussion where only the designated leader knows the answers to the questions; and the leader's job is to " lead " the group in a particular direction toward a particular solution or understanding. As this program was conceived, the leader felt that she had no way of knowing what each parent had to learn, what experience would be valuable for him. She had to become a member of the group in order to help each person assume his responsibility for his own growing. The leader did not stand up in front of the group. She sat with the other parents, thus symbolizing her feeling about the kind of leader she was and the fact that the responsibility for the group's actions and decisions lay with the group, not with her.

This leader consciously tried to be the best group member she could be. She seldom spoke as an expert or as one having authority. Rather, she tried to make her speaking a part of and a contribution to the group's thinking:

a. She clarified varying points of view so that the group could understand them better and deal with them.

b. She suggested a strategy, a way to help the group test a proposition or deal with a problem that seemed to be reaching no solution.

c. She asked a question that would test the validity of a statement or principle the group had adopted.

d. She tried to understand feelings. (" You feel that this situation has been unreal.")

e. She accepted any person's contribution which the group may have failed to recognize, by calling the group's attention to it. (" Marge has suggested that John was being manipulated by Jane in this role playing.")

f. Throughout the evening she tried to treat each parent as a person who was trying to be a good responsible group member.

This period of discussion, which took nearly one hour, was the time when the group " chewed over " the idea that was presented, questioned it, tried to understand it in a personal way . . . " What does this mean to me? "

The Analysis

The period of analysis, which took at least forty minutes, was the time when the group looked at its own functioning. Having spent considerable time and effort discussing the presentation, and trying to understand what had happened in the relationship of the people in the role-playing situation, the group members then tried to understand what was happening in their own group relationship. How well did they all talk to one stream of thought or was there much divergence; getting off the subject, side conversations between two or three people? Why were there side conversations? What was their effect on the group? Did the group accomplish anything as a group, arrive at any principles, get any new insights? Or was there no group product? Did the leader dominate the group, let it flounder, or help when it needed help? (How the group members felt about what she was doing and how she thought she was doing were sometimes two different things.) Was the group climate, the feeling among the members, friendly, indifferent, or hostile? (Different people had different perceptions of this, of course. The group then tried to understand why there were these different reactions to what was going on.)

This analysis sometimes involved the use of a check list (see page 140) which each person rated anonymously. The group then tallied the responses. At other times the analysis took the form of discussion in response to the questions asked by the leader, " How do we feel we functioned tonight, pretty well or not? " or, " What did we accomplish tonight; what was the important thing or things we learned? "

As the members of these parents' groups grew in their feeling of trusting each other, of belonging together, and of being friends, they began to apply the principles they had been discussing and the ideas they had been handling to the immediate personal life they had just experienced in the group meeting.

The Product

Invariably, by the third or fourth meeting, a mother or a father would say, " In our role playing we've been trying to learn how to understand the feelings that are behind people's words. I wonder how well we've been understanding *each other's* feelings while we were discussing them? " Or, " I felt for a time tonight as though I were dominating the group. I wonder how the rest of you felt? "

To the extent that a group has built up a relationship of trust, the members will respond with honesty and candor to such questions as these, secure in their feeling of being accepted here " no matter what I think," knowing that they will suffer no condemnation or loss of status or prestige with these, their friends, because the bonds between them are knit of personal respect and concern, one for another. Increasingly it will matter less and less to a group *and* to Mrs. Jones herself who Mrs. Jones *is* in this community, where she lives, how big her house is, and what position Mr. Jones holds. It only matters that Mr. and Mrs. Jones are growing as Christian persons and are practicing their new insights and skills in every relationship they have: with their children, with fellow employees, at church committee meetings, at union meetings, at the board meetings of the women's club or the business men's league.

It would be foolish to assume that a series of six meetings will produce Christian parents possessing all the skills of Christian living. What such a series can do is to increase the parents' sensitivity to the feelings behind the words and the behavior of all the members of the family, including themselves. In trying to become aware of the needs and tensions and concerns of their children, parents also begin to understand the struggles of each other and of themselves. As parents attempt to practice some of the skills they have learned and to use the insights they have gained, they discover that they are behaving less compulsively and that the living that goes on at home is more fun. Parents' meetings like these can, therefore, start families on a new path toward a more Christian home.

The parents who participated in this program wrote evaluative statements about the series at its close. Here are a few sample statements:

" We should have had six more. I was just getting started . . ."

" We finished every meeting when we got home, and often it took until one o'clock . . ."

". . . (this series) did more for our marriage than anything else the church has done."

". . . understand now why Terry can't be talked out of his notions. He feels manipulated, just like I do when Tom tries the same thing on me."

" We tried a family council in order to work at some of our problems. It seemed as though nothing was accomplished but a great airing of gripes and complaints, but we patiently *heard them all out* instead of ' shushing' them up, as we would have two months ago, and now a better feeling exists in our home than we've experienced in weeks."

Many churches are trying small group meetings that take various forms and follow various patterns and methods. How any teacher or leader or minister will work with a group of parents finally depends upon his or her own skills and time and convictions. The kind of programs for parents that helps them learn to live their Christianity seems, at this point, to be a valuable way for a church to use its leadership and a most helpful experience for families.

After one or two years of experience with the fall and spring series of parents' meetings, groups of parents may become "self-propelling groups" meeting throughout the year, setting their own schedule, subject matter, and so forth.

The Form of a Parents' Meeting

PROCEDURE	PURPOSE

1. **Present the subject** through one of the following methods or a plan of your own:
  a. Role playing
  b. Dialogue
  c. Planned skits
  d. Brief, cogent presentation by leader or qualified group member
  e. Case study (mimeographed for each person)
  f. Pamphlet material to be read beforehand as common preparation such as:[1]
    New Ways of Discipline by Dorothy Baruch
    Enjoy Your Child by James L. Hymes, Jr.
	1. To give a common experience and direction to the group at the beginning of the meeting.

2. **Discuss the subject;** question it; take hold of it.
    " What I think is. . . ."
    " I don't believe that's the way. . . ."
	2. The group "chews" over the idea at length, so each person can understand it and make it a part of his way of living with others.

[1] For other materials see page 174.

3. Analyze the total evening.
Group looks at itself; learns the relation of the " idea " being considered to the way the group members treated each other " here tonight." " In the role playing I didn't feel that Jane was really understanding what her neighbor was proposing. . . ." " That was the point I was trying to make way back there and *no one in this room understood me!* "

3. This results in growth in self-understanding (individual and group) and in a " we " experience, building a feeling of " we are a group and I belong. We are all in this thing together."

An Illustration of a Parents' Meeting

This is the third meeting of a six-meeting series for the parents of the nursery department of the church. The meeting began with a role-playing scene created by the group and enacted by two of the parents. The situation involved a husband and wife who were discussing money, where does it go, who spends what and why, and so on. Sylvia Brown and Henry Waters took the roles of Mary and Dick Jones in the scene; the other parents present were Tom and Jane Snow, Frank Brown, Henry and Miriam Waters, Ken and Bea Hough, Jim and Diane Sutton. The leader was Alice Todd.

The Discussion

Jane Snow: I felt that Dick Jones wasn't really understanding his wife.

Leader: How do you mean?

Jane Snow: She didn't really want a lot of "mad money" for herself each month just to buy new hats and things. She really wanted some to spend so she'd feel significant.

Henry Waters: Isn't ten dollars a month enough to make a woman feel significant? I don't spend that much a month on myself.

Jane: You don't understand what I mean.

Diane: No, no, she doesn't mean that. . . .

Henry: What do you mean then? I don't see how spending money makes you feel significant.

Diane: Oh, but it does.

Jane: What I mean is what I said. It isn't the amount of money a husband decides his wife shall have for her own that counts; it's working out the budget together that's important.

Leader: You believe, Jane, that if a husband and wife work out their spending together — this is our income and we'll spend this much for house, food, clothing, recreation, and so forth — even if there is nothing left for "mad money," she'll feel better than if the husband made all the money decisions and doled out a little or a lot to her.

Jane: That's right. And she'll be much more understanding of any unusual expenses that eat up the "mad money" or recreation money, or she'll work harder to help economize and save money for a down payment on something big if she's in on the planning.

Sylvia Brown: I was feeling — as the wife in the role playing — that I was being tolerated. Dick answered my questions, but I felt as though it was all a big bother to him. And when he said, "Here's ten dollars all for you. Buy a new hat, or take Sue to lunch, or do something fun" I felt as though he had said "there, there, nice kitty. I've petted you enough now. Take your catnip mouse and go away."

(General laughter which quickly subsided)

Diane: I was feeling the same way, watching it, Sylvia.

Ken Hough: But how can you explain *everything?* Insurance policies, interest payments on the mortgage, depreciation and up-keep on the car — it's complicated. I think most women can't under-stand it all, and don't want to.

Bea: I'm sure I don't want to. All I need to know is how much I can spend without getting called on the carpet.

Ken: Now, honey, I don't do that.

Leader: We have two points of view here, haven't we? One is that understanding how much money the family has and all the things it must be spent for, is too involved for most women and, in fact, they don't want to be bothered. Is that essentially what you said, Ken?

Ken: Yes, that's it.

Leader: And the other point of view — as I understand it — is something like this. It doesn't really matter if the wife — or the husband, for that matter — has a greater or lesser amount to spend on herself or himself. It matters more if *each* is included in the planning and in the decisions of how the family's money shall be spent. A wife needs to feel more an equal in the marriage than a well-kept member of the household.

Jim: I don't think a husband and wife have to do everything together in order to feel that they are equals. I go out to work every day and handle the money I earn. Diane takes care of the children and the house and makes all the decisions in those areas. From my point of view, we are equals.

Diane: Not everybody thinks the way you do, Jim. (She laughed, but not with mirth.)

Leader: Your idea is that a husband and wife can be equals by each one taking the responsibility for some area of the family life and not having to share with the other every bit of planning and deciding that goes on every day.

(Jim nods assent)

Tom: It seems to me that what we are getting at is not a method by which all families should live and spend their money, but a principle of living together that could exist in many methods. And let me take a crack at the principle. If each one feels that the other one — no, try again. Each one should be treated by the other one so that he feels important, worth while, and respected.

(A pause)

Bea: Isn't that true of every marriage or else it breaks up?

Tom: I don't think so. In some marriages one person dominates, the other acquiesces. Some marriages follow the pattern of the relationship of their parents, the husband behaves as his father did, the wife, like the mother.

Jane: And sometimes that's a devilish thing to work out.

Tom: Sometimes it is. (Jane and Tom laughed together as though they shared a joke or secret or experience apart from the group.)

Henry: Would you say then that there aren't many marriages of equals?

Tom: I don't know — but I suspect that that's true.

Frank: I don't get the point of this. We've been here an hour and a half now, and we haven't talked one word about our children. This is a nursery parents' meeting, isn't it? I don't get the connection.

Leader: You feel that talking about how a husband and wife

136

work out the problems of their budget is pretty far removed from understanding nursery children.

Frank: I sure do.

Sylvia: Maybe if we learned how to handle the budget . . .

Frank: I know that. What I need to know is why a three-year-old with new shoes will go right out and lose one within a week. Someone tell me that, and I'll feel as though my time was well spent tonight.

Jane: There could be lots of reasons for losing a shoe.

Miriam: No one could tell you that.

Leader: You feel that these meetings would be more profitable to you if we dealt with the problems we have with our children.

Frank: Yes, I do.

Jim: I think I understand what we're getting at, Frank. I'm not sure I agree with it . . . but perhaps it's this: the way a husband treats his wife, as an equal or not, is likely to be the way he treats his children.

Frank: But three-year-olds are not our equals. That's a bunch of poppycock. For my money, this new psychology that lets kids run all over you is wrong. It ruins the kid and would ruin me, too.

(Much response, side conversations, and so forth)

Tom: I'd like to try to answer that by going back to this principle I tried to state. We aren't trying to learn about budgets or specific problems with children. We're trying to learn an idea. Children, like everyone else, like to be treated as though they are important, valuable, worthy of the respect and love of their parents and the other members of the family.

Frank: I love my kids, but I don't include them in every decision I have to make.

Leader: Perhaps we aren't understanding each other. I'm sure Tom would agree that there are many decisions in a family's life that children cannot participate in wisely. Also, there are some decisions that concern the children, such as where and how to spend Sunday afternoon — these they should participate in. Not because the decision itself, in this case, is terribly important, but because the experience of being a valuable respected member of the family is.

Tom: That's what I've been trying to say. What matters is how the child feels about being important and loved, not what we parents think he should feel.

Diane: And so what matters is how the wife feels and not what the husband thinks she should feel?

Jane: That's right, Diane.

Leader: These feelings which we have observed and discussed tonight are a very real part of the personality of each of us. There is a phrase we will find useful in referring to them. To treat a child — or anyone — as a person means to live with him in such a way that he has a real sense of worth and belonging. Everyone longs to be treated as a person; everyone wants a deeply meaningful relationship to another, and yet be able to maintain his own integrity and individuality. Everyone wants to be useful to other persons and yet not be used by them.

The Analysis

In the analysis of the evening that followed this discussion, the group looked at itself quite self-consciously. Each member rated the group on the check list. They tallied the responses and they discussed the results.

Diane: I think the subject tonight was so real to some of us that we were a little hesitant to discuss it.

Henry: I was thinking that, too, Diane. Perhaps we should choose something a little more removed, and we'd be more free to talk about it.

Diane: Oh, I don't agree with that. I think this was good. I guess I didn't get my say in, but I got some things straightened out in my mind.

Jim: I'm confused about that item "leadership." I thought Mrs. Todd was the leader of the group and that she would take charge of the discussion, and we would learn what she planned. But that isn't right, is it, Mrs. Todd?

Frank: I don't understand that, either. I thought if I came to these meetings there would be a planned discussion about children's problems, and Mrs. Todd would know the answers. I think she knows the answers all right, but she won't tell us.

(The group laughed. Some relaxation in tension.)

Jane: Tom and I have tried to observe how you teach, and what you do to provide leadership, and we'd like to hear you say what you do.

Leader: (Good-humoredly) I didn't realize I was seeming so mysterious. I'm glad you told me. You must have felt as though I were letting you grope about with some ideas until some unknown moment when I would set forth the whole learning in one glorious lecture.

(General assent)

Well, that's not it.

In setting this series up, the committee felt that "Understanding What Makes for Good Human Relations" should be our series subject. I don't know all the things that are component parts of good human relations; I don't know how much each of you knows and what you must learn, but I do know that an "expert" lecturing is not good human relations. So I have not lectured, nor will I.

I feel that the best way I can teach is to help the group clarify its thinking, understand its feelings, suggest a next step when necessary, provide interpretations of words and ideas when such interpretations would be helpful. It is not my intention to direct your thinking along any set path to any particular conclusion. Each person will learn whatever is important for him to learn. I felt that one member of our group performed an excellent leadership function for us tonight by stating general principles for us to talk to instead of spending all of our time on specific human relations problems.

Jim: I noticed that, too. Tom did it, and it was very helpful.

Leader: The functions usually considered to be the job of the leader can, I believe, be shared, eventually, by the whole group. A group, like a family and like a democracy, becomes most productive when everyone shares in the responsibility for its life.

Diane: I think there were many unexpressed feelings in the group tonight — or anyway, not-understood feelings. Because of that, I feel this discussion is unfinished.

Ken: I do, too, Diane. I'd like to see a role-playing situation in which a husband and wife work out a budget together, even when she can't understand it.

Bea: I would, too.

Frank: I still feel as though we're fooling ourselves — thinking we're learning something. Are we afraid to deal with problems with our kids?

Leader: It has been the experience of previous nursery parent groups that it is hard to role play nursery children without "hamming it," Frank. But perhaps, next meeting, we could profitably study some anecdotal records of children and teachers at the nursery.

Frank: I wish we would do that.

Jane: Back to these unexpressed feelings. I think many of us were aware of some of the feelings at one time or another, but we don't know how to communicate the awareness, how to recognize another's feelings without embarrassing him or making him feel defensive.

Henry: That thought went through my head, too, Jane. Here's my wife — she hasn't said a thing all evening, and I can't figure out what she's feeling.

Miriam: I just couldn't think of anything to say. Guess I worked too hard today, and I'm too tired to think.

Leader: Let's remember that, too — for the next meeting. Jane, will you be the "rememberer" for us, and we'll try to work out some ways to express our own feelings and to understand another's feelings.

CHECK LIST FOR GROUP ANALYSIS OF A PARENTS' MEETING
THE MARKS OF CHRISTIAN GROUP LIFE

1. *Group Atmosphere or Feeling Tone* (*Group Climate*)

Superficial, cold, polite, " on our good behavior"	Sincere, warm, friendly, relaxed, accepting
People afraid to make contributions	People found it easy to join in

1	2	3	4	5	6	7

(What was the feeling in our group?)

2. *Group Sense of Direction*

Conversation hit and miss Much divergence and side-talk No agreement about the goal	Everyone knew what the goal was and tried to help the group toward it by relating his own and others' comments to the main stream of thought, clarifying ideas, and so forth

1	2	3	4	5	6	7

(How well did we " stay on the track? ")

140

3. Group Communication (Talking — Listening — Understanding)

It was hard to get your "say" in	Each member tried to be aware of all the ideas and feelings present and to keep them included in the group's thinking
Much polite listening; little understanding	
We talked past each other	

1	2	3	4	5	6	7

(How well did we really listen to and understand each other?)

4. Leadership

One person led the group (autocracy)	Everyone felt responsible for the group's progress and shared in the leadership by keeping aware of each member's contribution, helping the group "stay on the track," and so forth (democracy)
No one felt responsible for the group's activity (anarchy)	

1	2	3	4	5	6	7

(How responsible did the members feel for the group's functioning?)

5. Group Achievement

No apparent agreement on anything	We arrived at a common understanding or
Nothing accomplished	We created or achieved something as a group
Little growth in understanding new ideas or in group feeling	

1	2	3	4	5	6	7

(What did we get done?)

(Note: In using this check list with a group, the leader may say something like this: "Point one is the lowest end of the scale and seven the highest, indicating the best group feeling. You mark the scale at whatever point you feel describes how we did tonight. For example, if you feel that people were afraid to talk [under number one], you would check the lower end of the scale.")

FOR YOU TO THINK ABOUT

1. Study the responses of the leader in the illustration of a parents' meeting on page 134 and characterize each response in terms of what difference the response made in the group members' thinking and feeling. For example, did Mrs. Todd try to:

    a. understand someone's words and feelings? (so the group could also understand them)

    b. clarify the point under discussion or clarify another's remarks?

    c. mediate differences between two points of view?

    d. suggest strategy for proceeding in the discussion?

    e. raise a neglected point of view?

    f. summarize?

    g. furnish data, information?

    h. express her own ideas?

    i. other?

2. When were any of these functions of group interaction (dynamics) played by other members of the group?

3. As a group of parents becomes aware of how they are treating each other and becomes sensitive to each other's feelings, although unexpressed, they become more objective about how each is acting as a parent in a family. Which parents in the group do you feel are the most sensitive? What evidence is there?

PART FIVE

Growing in Wisdom and Humility

Finally, brethren, whatever is true, whatever is honorable, whatever is just, whatever is pure, whatever is lovely, whatever is gracious, if there is any excellence, if there is anything worthy of praise, think about these things. What you have learned and received and heard and seen in me, do; and the God of peace will be with you.

Philippians 4: 8, 9

CHAPTER TEN

The Teacher Looks at Herself

N<small>O</small> <small>TEACHER</small> ever feels that she has succeeded completely. Always she needs more time with the children, or more help in the room, or a better understanding of what she is doing and what needs to be done.

All of these matters are a rightful concern for a teachers' meeting, and oftentimes teachers, thinking together, can work out some plans both for the children and for their own behavior that will change the whole atmosphere of the nursery room as well as be of much greater help to a " William " or a " Jane."

Working through concerns such as these with the other teachers is good. It enlists the teachers' thinking in the specific problems and tasks of the nursery department and provides training for the teachers in how to think about and how to plan for particular children. It helps the teachers to understand more clearly what are valid religious experiences for the nursery child, and, at the same time, gives the teachers a method by which they can work to provide these for the children.

But each teacher, if she would keep growing in her skills and understanding of children, must also seriously and consistently engage in the pursuit of self-understanding and of the life God intends her to live.

How she will do this will be an individual decision for each teacher. Certainly, one way will be the diligent and faithful practice of prayer. She may have to learn how to pray. She will learn how by committing herself to the task. She may need help from others who are more skilled and more wise in prayer than she is, just as she needs help in her teaching. There are many books available that will be of real value to her.[1] Her minister also will be able to offer her help and suggestions.

Often prayer is not practiced, let alone practiced daily, because the person praying has no ideas or thoughts or concerns to pray about. She is not aware that, as she endures or experiences them, the little vexations, the sense of failure, the puzzlements that fill every day for every person, are all the proper concerns for prayer. As the ups and downs of the day occur, she may try to dispose of them herself — forgetting them or burying them — and then at night, if she remembers to pray, think only of " Now I lay me . . ." or " I'm glad this day is over. I'm tired, and will be grateful for a night's rest." If a teacher prepares herself to pray as she prepares an agenda of concerns for a teachers' meeting, the time spent in prayer will become much more enlightening and revitalizing.

Reading and studying the Bible is another way to prepare for prayer. Here, too, teachers feel discouraged about trying it. They do not know where to begin or where to stop. Some people follow the daily readings suggested by the American Bible Society; others take one book of the Bible and study it with the help of a good commentary, a few verses or a chapter at a time, wherever the break in thought occurs. Still others read the Bible where they want to and quit reading when they feel like it. The method does not matter so long as it is valuable and satisfying to the teacher who is reading. Unless she knows the Bible well, however, the first or the second method will probably prove more rewarding than the third.

It has been the testimony of Christians through the centuries that the individual daily practice of prayer is necessary to their continued growth and relationship to God; it is also true that the great strength and perseverance of the church, in both the first and the twentieth centuries, derive from equally faithful corporate worship. Teachers need both experiences; teachers often

[1] For some titles, see the listing in the bibliography on page 178.

have neither. If the nursery program is at the same hour as Sunday morning worship, or is an expanded session beginning before morning worship and continuing through it, for teachers to attend church worship services seems almost impossible.

Some churches have set up a late Sunday afternoon vesper service, once a month, particularly for the teachers of the church school. Other churches have tried to have enough teachers on the staff of each department of the church school so that, by taking turns, each teacher can attend a church service at least once a month. In actual practice, however, this often does not work out. Someone is sick or is out of town and the schedule breaks down; and shifting teachers has already been discussed as not desirable from the point of view of establishing an on-going relationship with the children.

Some of the larger Protestant churches in cities or in new communities have two or three services of Sunday morning worship, with a corresponding church school program and teaching staff during each worship hour. Although there are disadvantages in having one short hour for church school, the teachers do have an opportunity to attend one of the worship hours.

There may be a way to make up for this widespread lack of corporate worship experience. This way may be for the teacher to become a member of a small group of adults in the church who meet regularly to share their concerns about and their insights into living the Christian life. More and more churches are establishing such groups — called Christian Nurture Groups, Fellowship Groups, Religious Research Groups, and so forth. These groups are composed of men and women, sometimes couples, oftentimes not. Some of the groups undertake a systematic study of the Bible, or of church history, or of some current book dealing with a religious interpretation of life. Other groups spend their time together in a thoughtful discussion of whatever concern one of the members brings to the meeting. In these groups members often experience the depth of fellowship and a feeling of belonging to something of real significance that must have characterized the small bands of early Christians who met in homes.

The area of growth most difficult to undertake but, if undertaken, very rewarding personally in the search for the good life, is the area of self-understanding. Most of us do not understand ourselves very well: why we do and say some things that we really never intended to do or say; why we neglect to do other things which we really feel we should do; how we really are treating the people we live and work with; whether what we profess is actually what we are practicing. Such self-analysis is painful, but not impossible, especially with the help of some books currently available. *Peace of Mind* by Joshua L. Liebman, *Self-understanding* by Seward Hiltner, *Man's Search for Himself* by Rollo May, *The Mature Mind* by Harry A. Overstreet, are all very provocative of thought and introspection about one's self.

But whether a teacher reads books or not, it still would be wise for her to put some considered questions to herself.

Try working at a section of these questions during one of your periods of prayer and meditation. Consider them carefully, try to discover evidence to support the answer you have made. Ask yourself if your answer is more " wishful thinking " than actual practice.

If you don't know the answer to a question, keep it in mind as you work with children, or teachers, or parents, and you will begin to see yourself in action. You will slowly acquire an objectivity about yourself that will be a real means to further growth.

A. *As you work with children:*

Am I serving them or serving myself? Why do I feel this way?

What is my real motivation for doing this teaching and this work with parents?

What kinds of experiences provide my emotional satisfaction in this job? When Sunday morning does not go well, when I feel inadequate with a particular child, when I have been told to " go 'way " or " I don't like you," what do I do? How do I feel?

Are there some children I really do not like, and therefore do not love? Why? Is it because I feel defeated in dealing with them? Or has my feeling about their parents anything to do with it?

Which children am I failing? By recognizing this, what new understanding does this give me of myself?

For the most part, do I genuinely enjoy these children and myself when with them? What evidence have I?

B. *As you work with other teachers:*

What opportunities for growth am I providing them? In what ways are they becoming more competent with children? What steps have we, as teachers, taken together toward a better understanding and more faithful practice of Christianity?

Do we feel part of a team doing a job together or is it my "show" and they do what I suggest? How personally involved are they? (Writing down the preparation each teacher makes for each Sunday, what she does while there, and what she does to clean and straighten the room will help you think this through.)

What exciting and important things are we learning about children? How are we learning — by studying and working through our own experiences, or by someone more expert telling us?

C. *As you work with parents:*

How do I feel toward parents, in general and in particular? (How I feel about each one will give me a clue as to how I am treating each one.)

Do I strive continually to understand parents — all the parents — as persons trying to do the best they know? (This means I do not judge or condemn them, neither am I patronizing or superior in my attitude toward them.)

How am I performing my job — which is to be of help, of service, to provide ideas, to offer interpretations when asked for them?

Am I inclined to want to tell parents how to deal with their children, or to point out to them what their problems are and how to solve them? Cite the evidence.

How completely am I able to accept each of these parents? Whom do I reject? I wonder why?

D. *As you consider yourself:*

Am I growing toward Christian maturity myself? How do I know?

What are the marks of my progress?

What methods have I developed by which to take stock of my growth?

Two rather interesting methods, which teachers have discovered contribute greatly to their understanding of the progress they are making with their teaching and in their relationship to children, are worth noting here.

1. Select some trouble spot or perplexing situation, search out some clue that might help you to understand it, write the clue down, and try out for a month or two the line of action it suggests. For example, the trouble might be that the nursery hour is hectic; the clue is an earlier start. The statement is: " *If* I get the nursery room all set up *before* the first child arrives, I shall be able to spend more time with the children, do a better job of teaching, and feel less hectic when the hour is over." Date the statement, put it in your journal or curriculum material, or on your desk where you'll be reminded of it, and give it a try.

2. Keep a diary or journal about each Sunday morning, entering whatever seems important or perplexing or unsolved. Every two to three months, or whenever you want to, read back over the entries in the journal to see what progress you are making on your problems, or what is happening to the " difficult " children.

Some record, such as a diary or journal, can also be of great help in learning to pray. You may either write out prayers, listing the concerns that you want to pray about, or write out the questions and ideas that occur to you as you read and study the Bible. Re-reading these prayers, questions, ideas at regular intervals will become as instructive and revealing of the progress you are making in spiritual growth as the journal entries about the church school experience will be in your growth as a teacher.

PART SIX

Other Programs Within the Nursery Department

" So it is not the will of my Father who is in heaven that one of these little ones should perish."

Matthew 18: 14

" Let the children come to me, do not hinder them; for to such belongs the kingdom of God."

Mark 10: 14b

CHAPTER ELEVEN

Two-Year-Olds, Toddlers, and Babies

IT HAS BECOME almost a truism to say that the family, the home, is the primary religious institution. From the beginning of his life, through his relationships with his mother, father, sisters and brothers, the child learns to love by being loved. He comes to trust people, to accept them, to try to understand them, and to forgive them because he has found that his family, the people he knows best, are trustworthy, accepting, understanding, and forgiving with each other and with him.

The kind of living, the quality of the relationship — or simply, how his family members treat one another — becomes the core of the child's ideas about himself and his attitudes toward other people and the world. If he grows up in a family in which he is the " black sheep," he is very likely to spend his life either in hostile or antisocial acts toward the world of people which has so branded him, or in fearful withdrawal from society, expecting no concern, kindness, or respect and offering none.

This is just one illustration of how a child's *first* experiences do, in fact, become a basis for his understanding and behavior both toward himself and toward all other people. There are countless records and case studies to support this. Margaret Ribble, practicing psychiatrist; John Bowlby, psychoanalyst; and John Mac-Murray, philosopher, have come to the same conclusion from quite widely separated fields of thought and study.

This being true, churches ought seriously to consider expending time and money and leadership in a program of working with parents, helping them grow in understanding themselves and their children; providing for them resources in education, in friendship, in fellowship with each other, and in counseling; offering them opportunities, together with other families, to live and learn and have fun in family festivals, picnics, summer family camps, and other activities.

Such programs would undoubtedly be of greater value to the families involved and, from the church's point of view, a more effective way to help its people grow to Christian maturity, than trying to set up and operate a Sunday morning program for children under three so that their parents can go to church. The major business of a church ought to be its work with families rather than the care of two-year-olds, toddlers, and infants.

Many churches, however, do provide Sunday morning care for children under three during the worship hour, so that parents can go to church. If this is not the only relationship the church has with these families, and if the program provided is based on a sound understanding of the age group being cared for, this service will be much appreciated by the parents. For a thoughtful consideration of what it can offer these children, let us take a closer look at them, what they are like, how they are growing, what their needs are.

From Two to Three

This is the age child about whom adults are inclined to say, " What a cute little boy (or girl)! ", only to have the child stop cold in his tracks, look up from his clay pounding or stop the racing motor on his blue " Ford," and assert, in such a manner that you know well not to contradict, " *I'm* not a little boy. I'm a *big* boy." And that's probably the best clue to his behavior.

The two-year-old has just recently found his Self. He has sorted it out from his mother, father, older brothers or sisters, and anyone else who comprises the family; and he is quite happy about the whole thing. He, like all the rest of us, is not quite sure, however, just what his Self is like, how important it is, what it can do, and almost his every word and action is an effort, in his own mind, to find out more about himself as a person. Many of the characteristics we normally associate with " two-year-oldness " can be understood when we recognize this.

The two-year-old is an imitator. He tries to do everything he sees an older brother or sister do. He accepts success or failure as another clue to his Self. (" I want to do it, too; I'm big enough! " or, " I can't do that, Daddy. I'm not big enough.") Adults say of him that he is negative, stubborn. But here, too, he is discovering something about himself, how important he is, what decisions he will be allowed to make if he insists, whether he can make big people do what he wants them to do. Probably the two-year-old's most frequently used sentence is the demand that he be treated as an independent person with intentions and abilities all his own, " I want to do it mySELF! "

The two-year-old's Self includes more than his physical person. It also includes his clothes, his toys, his spoon, cup, dish, bed, blanket — in fact, everything that has been a consistent part of his environment. Whenever anyone comes close to, picks up, or carries off any of these possessions, his Self is threatened, even attacked, and he cries out with vigor, " That's mine! " He usually persists in this until he gets that part of his Self back, or mother comes to the rescue, or his attention is diverted, an artifice less and less easy to use.

This emerging Self is the core of the developmental tasks of the two-year-old. Each new social, physical, intellectual accomplishment serves to enhance or clarify his Self. It is easy to see, therefore, that in his social life, in playing with other children, it is next to impossible for the two-year-old to let anyone else handle or play with his possessions. His possessions are part of his Self, and having just begun to find his Self, he cannot possibly give it away. There is no more sense in trying to " teach " a child from two to three to share in this sense, than there is in trying to teach a child to walk before he has learned to balance himself standing. Each person has to be quite sure he has a Self before he can consider giving it away. The two-year-old has to live with his Self, including his possessions, in a non-threatening environment for some months until he himself gradually comes to discover that he is no less a Self for having allowed his friend to hold his doll or ride his truck. This insight is not born overnight. It is part of the process of growing up, and most of us are still working on the same problem with different possessions — money, or leadership, or personal service — which we think we cannot afford to part with or find time to offer to others.

The two-year-old is a social creature. He likes children about him although he does not really play with them. His play is called " parallel play " or " presence play." That is, he carries on his activity in the presence of another child; he does not take part in a mutually agreed-upon activity, such as building part of a block road, or being the daddy in playing house. On occasion he may follow the directions of an older child, but this usually does not last very long. He gets tired and goes off on his own.

Strange children usually do not arouse any reaction in the two-year-old except curiosity. Strange adults may make him fearful, unhappy, panicky, depending upon myriads of circumstances and his past experiences. From losing fear of people to approaching them with trust and delight is a long way to grow; and this, like the matter of sharing, cannot be hurried; nor can we skip steps in the process. We can help the child in the process, but we cannot do his growing for him. To leave a fearful, crying child in a new and strange situation, such as his room at church, on the theory that he will cry it out and get over it, is more likely to increase his fear of new situations than to give him the help he needs to handle them.

Rather, the two-year-old needs love, he needs help, he needs protection from the strong and powerful adult Selves that surround him, until he finds that he really is adequate to meet the situation just as " They " believed he could. And above all, he needs time. We don't know his time schedule for growth. All we know is that for every person it is different, and it is always uneven. It goes in fits and starts. When the two-year-old is ready to take the step, any step, he will let us know; that is, if we don't urge him, push him, hurry him, make him lose confidence in himself. " I can do it mySELF! "

Two-year-olds develop delightful imaginations about their toys, themselves, what they have done. Ricky, at thirty months, discovered the wonderful fact that the world is full of bugs. He could pick them up, and carry them about, and cover them with sand, and walk them up legs of his jeans; while his big brother watched almost admiringly, and his mother was both amazed and amused. On successive days Ricky found a ladybug which he said was " awful tired," a little black beetle, a huge black ant, a June bug, and an angleworm. Each evening he played that he was the bug of the day. He tried to do the things he had made the much-manipulated bugs do, to the amusement of his family and to his own great delight. The two-year-old's animals and bed toys often take on personality and he talks to them and treats them as he feels he has been treated — a most revealing experience to a mother trying to be good and wise.

Another aspect of his intellectual development is his growing awareness of physical relationship. He finds great joy in putting things together, such as simple puzzles, and objects that are made to fit in specific and understandable fashion. He usually does not want help. " I can do it mySELF! "

Time has little meaning to him. He lives in the " Here " and the " Now." To tell him that he can have a cookie after his nap or that he can go home after church is over is almost the same thing, in his mind, as saying, " No, you can't do it." It might never happen, for all he knows. One tot, who was approaching three, was beginning to understand her mother's response " after a bit " as meaning " pretty soon " or " as soon as I'm finished here." One day her cookie request was answered with " after a while." She stamped her foot and almost shouted at her bewildered mother, " No. After a bit."

There is as much variation in the physical development of children two to three as there is in any other aspect of their growth. Perhaps in this area the variations are more readily observed. Generally, there is little small-muscle development or co-ordination, which means two-year-olds usually cannot cut, or string beads, or pour from a pitcher into a cup, or perform many other skills requiring much co-ordination. Two-year-olds usually go up and down stairs one foot at a time. Some time, between two and three, many of them master the co-ordination required to pedal and steer their "trikes." Most two-year-olds are toilet-trained soon after their second birthday, although accidents, especially under strain or during great concentration, are usual.

Language is important to the two-year-old. This age uses many baby sounds, reversed and substituted consonants, and three-syllable words reduced to one syllable; but he will keep trying to be understood, usually without anger or annoyance, repeating as often as he is asked, and patiently answering questions about what he is saying. And when he finally is understood, he is as pleased with the adult as he is with himself.

The emotional development of the two-year-old — how he handles frustration, disappointment, anger, attack — can be easily described. Usually he cries, or yells, or wails. These noises convey specific meanings to his mother; but to a sitter, a teacher, or a stranger, the meanings are hard to distinguish. The two-year-old really does not know how to handle disappointment, fear, frustration, or physical hurt other than to cry out, which usually brings adult help. But gradually he learns some things about cause and effect, what makes what happen, and one day he will back the wagon up to free the wheel from the fence post instead of continuing to pull at it and yell furiously. And another day instead of crying he will *call*, "Mommy, help me! It's stuck and I can't undo it!"

There are three outstanding aspects of the two-year-old's religious development. If his life at home has been happy, if he has been physically cared for, loved, and feels secure in his relationships with the members of his family, he can both receive and return affection. Some children, who do not know love and security, can neither accept affection nor return it, although they long deeply to do both. If in their early years they have habitually experienced rejection, or impersonal physical care, or inconsistent treatment, they build a strong defense about themselves and look on the world of people with distrust and suspicion. These children can only be saved by a constant loving, forgiving, understanding relationship with an adult whom they come to trust.

Given the experience of being part of a happy home, the second aspect of the two-year-old's religious development is that all his energies flow out from him into the world about him. He has no conscious awareness that people need his help, or that he is a part of all mankind or any such thing; but he is an active, working, participating member of the life about him, in the world of things and of people. He wants to belong to his world, he struggles to keep up with it, and he spends his daily quota of energy bent on understanding it. This is the first step along the path that leads to a conscious decision to live one's life in the service of men and of God.

A third characteristic of the two-year-old, which is another first step toward Christian maturity, is his delight in and enthusiasm for new experiences, such as throwing stones in the lake and hearing them go " galump "; new wonders, such as bugs; new treats, such as ice cream cones for dessert. The world is new and wonderful to him, and each day has its glories. This could be true of adults. It should be. But our minds, so often, are so concerned with the cares and trivia of home and work that we fail to notice that the lilies of the valley have little white bells on them or the pigeons eating peanuts on the street corner really " have awfully pretty blue feathers and pink feet." If the adults about him do not greet his delight with amused laughter or an unenthusiastic response, the two-year-old can and will continue to discover that he lives in a world that abounds with evidences of God's love and care for men, all men, himself included.

A church that intends to set up a program for two-year-olds should do it with full awareness of the characteristics of this age child, and develop the plans and program so that it will be the best possible experience for the child. Here are some minimum essentials for this program.

1. Two-year-olds need space, 35 square feet per child is a minimum, with no more than twelve children to the room. The room should be equipped to suit the skills and interests of this age child. It should be warm, well-ventilated, light, close to toilet facilities, clean, attractive, and on the first floor. There should be pictures of subjects that interest the children hung on the wall at the children's eye level. Pictures which are inexpensive, that can be changed for others when the children's interest indicates the need for this, are preferable. Bright curtains, a few painted chairs (one for every child is not needed), and a table about 18 inches high, linoleum or asphalt tile floor, and a 9 x 12 rug in one corner for looking at books and working puzzles are basic furnishings. Equipment should be sturdy with no sharp edges and should include as much of the following as possible: a ball to roll; pull and push toys; dolls and cuddly toys that can be washed weekly; a bouncing horse and a rocking horse, a rocking boat, a walking board, and a low platform with two steps up and two steps down; large crayons and paper and paste at the work table; picture books and a few simple puzzles; a tea table (child size — not toy size), dishes, cupboard, stove, highchair for a doll; building blocks to make towers and roads (no fancy shapes are necessary), a truck and a small wagon that can be loaded and dumped, and a few other cars; a block stack; a pounding toy; a toy that permits fitting blocks of certain colors and shapes into certain holes; and possibly a piano.

2. The adults in charge should be *teachers* who know what two-year-olds are like, what their developmental tasks are, what teaching them means. The adults should not be " sitters " or think of themselves as " sitters." There should be one adult for every six children, and always two adults present so that one will be free at any time to help a child who may require the teacher's full attention.

3. The entire morning's program is individual in nature. Each child uses whatever in the room appeals to him for as long as he is interested. No group activity is ever planned for these children, for they are still in the stage of parallel play. There may need

to be a time for toileting, for juice and a cracker, and perhaps for rest, depending on what part of the morning and for how long the children are in the church.

4. A pleasant, secure, affectionate relationship between teacher and child is the basis for the teaching-learning-growing that can take place in this program, just as it is in the group for three-year-olds. Parents should stay with the child until he is ready for them to leave, and parents should be easily and quickly available if they are needed. If a child consistently cries or fusses when his parent leaves, it is a signal that the child is not yet ready for separation from his parents. The parents should wait a little longer before bringing the child to the church. As with all pre-school children, the two-year-old must feel secure and happy in his church. If he does not, the good quality of all the rest of his church school experience will depend upon his surmounting this first unhappiness.

5. As with all preschool groups, if this program cannot be done adequately with the welfare of the child in mind, it would be better not to do it at all.

Toddlers — From Walking to Two Years Old

The outstanding characteristic of these children is the almost complete use of their energies in physical accomplishment: learning to walk, to get up from the floor, to reach for something from a standing position, to pull a toy or to push one. They also are trying to talk, to feed themselves, and many of the girls from eighteen months to two years of age are quite successfully accomplishing toilet-training. (An equal number — or more — are not.) The obvious developmental tasks of this age group are almost entirely physical.

Although the toddler is growing in all the same ways, along the same paths that we have described for the three-year-old and for the two-year-old, his home can provide everything he needs for the continuance of this growth. His needs are simple; his abilities and accomplishments are simple. We are not very sure just exactly what his understanding of himself, his family, the world is. The thing we know for a certainty is that his greatest need, and the greatest aid to this growth and development in all aspects of growing, is consistent, good, loving care. It is doubtful whether anyone can provide this love as well as the child's mother and his family.

If a church does set up a program for toddlers, a good policy, and one that makes this kind of program valuable for parents, is to have a pre-enrollment conference between the parents of the toddler and the leader of the group, and regular conferences thereafter. Toddlers, like all preschool children, differ greatly in their readiness to be separated from their mothers. At the pre-enrollment conference the leader and the parents should discuss this, as well as other aspects of the toddlers' program, and the church's philosophy about young children. Subsequent conferences would follow the general plan or purpose for home visits set forth in chapter six.

If a program for toddlers is undertaken by the church, the following are essential features.

1. The room should provide a minimum of 35 square feet of floor space for each child, no more than eight children to a room, no fewer than two adults. The adults should be understanding, loving people; gentle and soft-spoken; equipped with much patience, some diapers, and a few changes of toddler-size clothes. There should be bathroom facilities close by; the room should be cheerful and clean, located on the first floor. Here, too, children should never be left crying, and their parents should always be quickly available.

2. All equipment should be washable, and none of it small enough for a child to swallow. It is very important to be sure that the paint used on any articles is nontoxic. Depending upon the number and abilities of the children, the room may need one or more play pens. Some cuddly toys, some rubber toys that squawk, some push and pull toys, some pans and wooden spoons, rattles, standard nursery size blocks, and some little blocks to put into the pans or just to carry about are recommended.

3. At its best this program can be a satisfactory experience for

the children who are happy in it and a real service to their parents. If it is less than this, the church had better not undertake it.

Babies

In some respects the crib room for babies is a service more easily provided for parents than is the program for toddlers, twos, and threes. It may be easier to find a warm, understanding, faithful person for this job than it is to find qualified teachers for children who are a little older. Too, it seems to adults that babies are not as emotionally disturbed by strange places, strange people, and separation from their mothers as are older brothers and sisters.

But this may not be true. What Margaret Ribble found in her long study and observation of infants suggests that it may be more nearly correct to say that we do not know how a crib room experience affects infants rather than to say that it does not affect them.

Care of babies in cribs is a great responsibility which requires no less adequate health and safety precautions than hospitals practice in their nurseries. Cribs and bassinets must be washed after each use; sheets and diapers should be sterile and available in good supply; strict standards against accepting babies with any signs of ill health or infection should be in force. Churches operating this program need to be aware of any board of health regulations that govern setting up and operating nurseries for babies.

Many churches feel that only a trained nurse should be in charge of the nursery. Whoever is in charge should have at least one assistant. It is important with this age, too, that the same adults care for the infants each Sunday. Staffing this room by " drafting " some mother who came to church to worship, is to be deplored on two counts, on both the mother's and the babies'.

This is an expensive sitting service. Some churches can afford it, and some parents of young babies want to use it. The churches who do provide crib rooms should recognize that this is only a part of their ministry to young parents. The churches that cannot afford this service can find other ways of serving their parents such as the following:

1. It may be possible for a local radio station to broadcast the worship services, so parents can listen at home and still care for their baby.

2. Two or three neighbors within a few blocks of each other might alternate being sitters, one family having two or three infants one Sunday and then spend one or two successive Sundays in church. The church nursery visitor can help to set up these plans.

3. Members of the older adult church school classes may undertake a service project of free sitting in their homes for young parents during the church hour. Here, too, someone from the nursery department should help work out the arrangements.

4. The church may be able to conduct two successive worship services on Sunday mornings so that in turn each of the parents can attend.

FOR YOU TO THINK ABOUT

1. In what ways is the home the primary religious institution? For young children, then, what can the church offer?

2. Make a plan for a room for eight two-year-olds, locating coat hooks, bathroom facilities, and essential equipment.

3. What would you, the teacher, say to parents who are going to leave with you a crying two-year-old, with the comment, " He'll be all right after a while. He always gets over it in time."

CHAPTER TWELVE

The Church-Sponsored Weekday Nursery School

A SIGNIFICANT PROGRAM for nursery children and their families is the church-sponsored weekday nursery school. This is a program, usually for three- and four-year-olds, which is set up and directed according to the standards of nursery school education. It ordinarily operates for two and a half to three hours each morning, five days a week.

There are a number of reasons why church-sponsored weekday nursery school programs are growing in popularity. The many nurseries and day-care centers set up during the last war, mostly to accommodate working mothers with young children, awakened great interest in the nursery school movement. A number of these child-care centers made the professionally trained nursery school educator weep inside for the children who needed more help with their fears, inadequacies, and hostilities than the center could provide. Nonetheless, the fact that they operated, and operated well for the most part, convinced many people that education at the nursery school level could be a valuable experience for a child, an experience which his home and his neighborhood, no matter how wise and excellent, probably could not duplicate. Whereas, two and three decades ago, nursery schools were considered by most people to be private and expensive " play schools " where the rich could place their children to learn good manners and at the same time give the mothers mornings off from their children; now many families quite actively seek nursery schools for the valuable learning and growing experiences they provide for children.

There are other reasons why nursery schools are gaining in popularity. Mothers do need some time off, and parents with young children do need emotional support and wisdom about children, and friendship with other families where there are young children. All of these the church-sponsored nursery school can provide for families. Because the nursery school can become the basis for a very valuable church-family relationship, many churches have come to feel that the nursery school program is as valuable an extension and expansion of the total religious education effort as the summer vacation church school program for older children has long since proved itself to be. Like the vacation church school, the nursery school has the advantage of many hours each week with each child, for the nursery school offers as many as sixteen hours weekly throughout the school year. In the life of the child the church probably will not again have such sustained contact with the child or such close personal relationship with his parents.

Nursery school education, because it is not primarily concerned with facts and bits and pieces of information, which the pupil must "learn" and then convince his teachers that he has "learned," actually operates, with children and with their parents, on principles that we have already described as fundamental to religious living. That is, the educational philosophy of nursery schools — that each child is unique, his needs are specific for him, the steps he can take in his learning and growing only he can determine; and that the job of the teacher is to help each child work out *his* problem, take *his* step, grow in *his* chosen direction, not hers — implies a conviction that each child is a person of intrinsic worth.

This educational point of view also implies that the relationship which will permit the child to grow in confidence, adequacy, and trust is one in which the teacher constantly strives to understand behavior, not to judge it; to be sensitive to the child's needs, not to use him to serve hers; to help him discover his own Self, not to mold him into the Self she thinks he should be.

Both this conviction about the value of personality and this

166

understanding of the relationship which must exist between persons, if each is to live life in terms of his own talents and creativeness, are related to the doctrine the church has always proclaimed: that man is created in the image of God. Therefore, every person has great worth; human life is not to be held cheap, nor is it to be scarred, tampered with, or manipulated by other human life; for in doing so the creative spirit, which is of God, within human lives wilts and is buried deep. If the chief end of man is to glorify God, then man's words, his actions, his every moment must reveal the spirit of God within him, must be true to the nature of God insofar as man can understand what that nature is.

Such an educational philosophy creates a learning environment which is essentially Christian. Whatever the child learns of right and wrong, of justice and fair play, of regard for the rights and feelings of others, and whatever ideas and concepts he comes to hold about himself, the kind of person he is — all of this learning takes place against a backdrop of Christian understanding and conviction.

The Program for Parents

The program for parents that is part of the church-sponsored nursery school operates on the same educational philosophy as the nursery school itself; namely, that each parent's needs are different, known only to him, and he must do his own learning and growing. Accepting this premise makes the traditional type of parents' meetings (fifty adults invited to hear a talk, see a film, scan an exhibit, browse through new books, drink a cup of coffee, and go home) clearly not the only way to help these parents grow.

In large part, the relationship must be an individual, personal one between the nursery school teacher and the parents, just as exists in the nursery school itself between the teacher and the children. How this relationship will be carried on depends on the teacher's skills, time, and convictions, as well as on the parents' willingness to participate in the relationship. Certainly regular evening conferences in the homes of the children when both parents can be present are valuable to both parents and teachers. Giving both parents an opportunity to make observations in the nursery school (fathers on Sunday, if they can't attend during the week), followed immediately by a luncheon conference with the teacher, has proved to be a very helpful experience for many parents. Some schools have been very successful in operating a co-operative system in which the mothers take turns, by schedule, helping the trained teachers of the school; thus cutting the costs of operation and providing real opportunities for parents to learn about children. The maximum benefits to the mothers, with minimum insecurity for the children, who are not always able to " share " their mothers with other children, comes when " helping " mothers and the head teacher meet in regular staff sessions for preparation and evaluation. Without such instruction and discussion much real learning is lost for the mothers.

Parents' meetings for groups of parents are as necessary, however, as is the individual teacher-family relationship, and for some, may be more valuable. Churches have carried out all the kinds of meetings described in chapters eight and nine. Those described in chapter nine, " Meetings to Help Parents Grow Toward Christian Maturity," have proved particularly valuable, both to parents and to the church, if the nursery teacher is skilled enough to undertake them.

This nursery school parents' program, if it is done well, can be one of the most effective services the church extends to the community. But it must be done well, else it becomes for the parents just another item on an already too full calendar of activities.

Getting Started

The staff for a weekday nursery school program should be in the ratio of one teacher for eight children, never fewer than two teachers for a group. The head teacher, or director, should be a person trained in nursery school education and a sincere, committed Christian. She — or he — should fulfill the descriptions of the nursery teacher found in chapters two, four, and ten. She should be able to establish a person-to-person, " I-Thou " relationship with all people — because she is that kind of person herself. She should know the Christian beliefs that are the basis for such a way of living with people, and she should observe the practices of Christian people in prayer and worship in order to grow herself.

If the school can afford it, and if they can be found, it would be well to have all the teachers so trained and so dedicated. Many churches cannot afford this, however, so various solutions have been found for securing adequate leadership. Some schools have used lay women from the church community who are mature Christians and who have an educational background and experience. These persons have been trained as permanent assistants in the school. Other schools have been fortunate enough to secure students from a neighboring educational institution who fulfill their practice teaching requirements by working as assistants in the school. A third solution, already mentioned, is the one of having the mothers of the children themselves take turns assisting in the school. There is no best way to staff a school. Any of these suggestions can be very satisfactory. What matters is that whoever serves as a teacher be loving and become wise.

Selecting the families to be enrolled in the school should be done in a conference between the teacher and the family applying. Since this program is for children and their parents, the parents will want to know what their part in it is, as well as what the children's part is like. Parents should know about the regular conference schedule, the quarterly observation schedule, when parents spend a morning observing in the nursery school, the work nights, the parents' meetings during the year. If parents know ahead of time what is expected of them, they will be prepared for their responsibilities; and if they feel they cannot fulfill these, they will be free not to obligate themselves by enrolling their child in the program.

The financing of the nursery school program has, like the problem of staffing and selecting the applicants, been solved in many different ways. The best solution is for the nursery school program to be considered an integral part of the work and ministry of the church. The board of trustees includes it in the annual budget, assuming the total cost of operating it, collecting the tuition fees, and underwriting whatever deficit there may be.

This is the best way, but not the only way. Another pattern is for the church to assume the expense of light, heat, janitor service, and physical upkeep. The other budget items are salaries, expense account for the director, operating expenses (juice, crackers, crayons, paper, paint, and so forth), and equipment fund (for repair and replacement of the large, durable items). When these are added up and divided by the number of pupils in the school, the quotient is the tuition per pupil. If the figure is above the ability of the families of the community to pay, other funds must obviously be found. Sometimes the board or committee of Christian education includes an item for the nursery school in the yearly budget for Christian education. Some schools have been fortunate enough to be given small endowments or trust funds by the more wealthy members of the church to be used for the equipment fund. Still others have had their parents raise the necessary deficit by bake sales, rummage sales, children's clothing sales, concerts, and so forth.

The Physical Environment and the Program

Before a church undertakes a nursery school program, however, it should first consider the space and facilities required. A nursery school requires indoor play space of from 30 to 50 square feet per child enrolled (the more space, the better), plus a large open indoor space for rhythms, bike riding, skipping, and running when the weather does not permit outdoor play. The outdoor play space of 75 to 100 square feet per child should be safe from traffic and other hazards, well-drained, partly shady, directly outside one door of the school. There should be some hard surface in the outdoor play area for wheel toys, climbing equipment, one or two swings, a sandbox; and space to plant, or dig, or make mud pies, or " pick dandelions." In other words, a place where children and the good earth can come together in happy exploration and imaginative delight. (" Teacher, I'm going to dig to China! " or, " Look what I found! A bug with no head and no legs! What a funny bug.")

The indoor space should be light, cheerful, clean, warm on the floors, with windows low enough for children to look out, preferably on the first floor of the building. The floors and furnishings of the room need to be of a kind that can be cared for easily with a minimum of effort by teachers and janitors. The furniture should be sturdy, of a size to fit the nursery school child. Bathroom facilities, either sized to fit or equipped with small seats and stepstools, should be near at hand with one toilet and one washbowl for every eight to ten children. There should be individual locker space for each child and a room for isolation in case a child becomes ill during the morning.

If such space as this is available, information about furniture and equipment can be found in a number of publications. References are listed in the bibliography. The equipment need not be fancy or expensive. Much of it can be made if the parents and the church have the time to do this. Buying all the equipment from nursery school educational supply houses is a very costly undertaking for the initial investment; and in not a few cases, the imagination and work of fathers and mothers in constructing hollow blocks, stoves, beds, cupboards, and refrigerators produces better, sturdier equipment than can be purchased.

Many states have quite specific regulations concerning the operation of nursery schools, and both state and local boards of health have set up rules governing health examinations and readmission to school by doctor's certification after an illness. Churches intending to set up a nursery school should make themselves cognizant of these laws and regulations and be prepared to meet the standards the laws establish.

The morning program for the nursery school includes indoor and outdoor play, toileting, rest, juice and crackers. There are almost limitless activities possible in the free play period, both indoors and outdoors, and there are many nursery school textbooks, describing these in detail. The bibliography lists a number of these. What activities actually take place depend on the teachers, the equipment available, and the background and experience of the children.

The Religious Foundation

There was a time in the history of the church in the United States when the education of children was under the direction and influence of the church. This is no longer true. In the matter of public education, most Protestants strongly support the doctrine of the separation of church and state. Much good has come from this; other good often lies stillborn. Too few schools hold as an explicit, major goal of their educational effort that each child shall grow increasingly in self-understanding, that he shall experience personhood and thus come to treat other people as persons, that he shall discover that his life is part of all the lives about him, and that he is responsible to God both for his own well-being and for that of his brothers.

A church-sponsored nursery school cannot "teach" three-year-olds such weighty concepts, of course. But these are the concepts that operate in a good church-sponsored nursery school program, that underlie the experiences of the teachers, the children, and their parents; and some of the parents will grasp them with the enthusiasm of a convert. These ideas are powerful ones, and when they operate in the lives of the adults with whom the child lives, the kind of living that takes place changes, with positive consequences for the life of each child and for the lives of all with whom he has relationships.

By such a church-sponsored nursery school program the church once again can have great influence in the lives of children and adults; not an influence springing from doctrine, dogma, or ritual, but an influence that opens the door to the abundant life of love and trust and freedom which God intends for all men.

FOR YOU TO THINK ABOUT

1. What are the unique contributions that the church-sponsored nursery school can make to the growth of the young child?

2. What contributions can such a program make to the parents of these children?

3. Should your church consider operating a nursery school? Why or why not?

Bibliography

GENERAL REFERENCES

BOOKS

Bowlby, John, *Child Care and the Growth of Love* (London: Whitefriars Press, Ltd.). (A Pelican Book published by Penguin Books.)

Eakin, Mildred M. and Frank, *Your Child's Religion* (New York: The Macmillan Company).

Gesell, Arnold and Ilg, Frances L., *Infant and Child in the Culture of Today* (New York: Harper & Brothers).

Howe, Reuel L., *Man's Need and God's Action* (Greenwich: The Seabury Press).

Hymes, James L., Jr., *A Child Development Point of View* (New York: Prentice-Hall).

———, *Understanding Your Child* (New York: Prentice-Hall).

Miller, Randolph Crump, *The Clue to Christian Education* (New York: Charles Scribner's Sons).

Miller, Samuel H., *The Life of the Soul* (New York: Harper & Brothers).

Sherrill, Lewis J., *The Gift of Power* (New York: The Macmillan Company).

———, *The Struggle of the Soul* (New York: The Macmillan Company).

PERIODICALS

Child Study. Child Study Association of America, 132 East 74th Street, New York 21, New York.

Childhood Education. The Association for Childhood Education International, 1200 15th Street, N. W., Washington 5, D. C.

International Journal of Religious Education. 79 East Adams Street, Chicago 3, Illinois.

GENERAL REFERENCES FOR PARENTS

BOOKS

Arnold, Arnold, *How to Play With Your Child* (New York: Ballantine Books).

Duff, Annis, " *Bequest of Wings,*" *A Family's Pleasures With Books* (New York: The Viking Press).

Garrison, Charlotte Gano and Sheehy, Emma Dickson, *At Home With Children* (New York: Henry Holt & Co.).

Hymes, James L., Jr., *Understanding Your Child* (New York: Prentice-Hall).

Spock, Benjamin, *Baby and Child Care* (New York: Pocket Books, Inc.).

PAMPHLETS

Baruch, Dorothy W., *How to Discipline Your Children*. Public Affairs Committee, 22 East 38th Street, New York 16, New York.

Hymes, James L., Jr., *Being a Good Parent*. Parent Teacher Series, Bureau of Publications, Teachers College, Columbia University, New York 27, New York.

———, *Discipline*. Parent Teacher Series, Bureau of Publications, Teachers College, Columbia University, New York 27, New York.

———, *Enjoy Your Child — Ages One, Two and Three*. Public Affairs Committee, 22 East 38th Street, New York 16, New York.

Neisser, Edith, *Making the Grade as Dad*. Public Affairs Committee, 22 East 38th Street, New York 16, New York.

Wishik, Samuel M., *How to Help the Handicapped Child*. Public Affairs Committee, 22 East 38th Street, New York 16, New York.

PERIODICALS

Child Study. Quarterly. Child Study Association of America, 132 East 47th Street, New York 21, New York.

Parents' Magazine. 52 Vanderbilt Avenue, New York 17, New York.

Two to Six. 420 Madison Avenue, New York 17, New York.

CHAPTER ONE

BOOKS

Allport, Gordon W., *The Individual and His Religion* (New York: The Macmillan Company).

Campbell, Elizabeth W., *Security for Young Children: The Foundation for Spiritual Values* (Boston: Pilgrim Press).

Mitchell, Lucy Sprague (ed.), *Another Here and Now Story Book* (New York: E. P. Dutton & Co., Inc.).

Rudolph, Marguerita, *Living and Learning in Nursery School* (New York: Harper & Brothers).

PAMPHLETS

Havighurst, Robert J., *Developmental Tasks and Education* (New York: Longmans, Green & Co., Inc.).

CHAPTER TWO

BOOKS

Buber, Martin, *I and Thou* (New York: Charles Scribner's Sons).

Sherrill, Lewis J., *The Gift of Power* (New York: The Macmillan Company).

———, *The Struggle of the Soul* (New York: The Macmillan Company).

LEAFLETS

Nicely, Sally K., *Men Needed for the Pre-School Departments.* National Council of Churches of Christ, Office of Publication and Distribution, 120 East 23rd Street, New York 10, New York.

Chapter Three

BOOKS

Adair, Thelma and McCort, Elizabeth, *How to Make Church School Equipment* (Philadelphia: Westminster Press).

Long, Grayce E., *Laughter and Song* (Boston: Boston Music Company).

MacCarteney, Laura, *Songs for the Nursery School* (Boston: Boston Music Company, 116 Boylston Street).

Read, Katherine, *The Nursery School: A Human Relationships Laboratory* (Philadelphia: W. B. Saunders Co.).

PAMPHLETS

Conover, E. M., *The Church School and Parish House Building.* National Council of Churches of Christ, Office of Publication and Distribution, 120 East 23rd Street, New York 10, New York.

Equipment and Supplies. Association for Childhood Education International, 1200 15th Street, N. W., Washington 5, D. C.

Kramer, Emma Jane, *Equipment and Arrangement for Children's Groups in the Church* (Nashville: Abingdon Press).

LEAFLETS

The Church's Ministry to Nursery Children and Their Family. National Council of Churches of Christ, Office of Publication and Distribution, 120 East 23rd Street, New York 10, New York. Write for information about available titles in this series.

Nicolaysen, Mary, *Art Activities in the Nursery Program.* National Council of Churches of Christ, Office of Publication and Distribution, 120 East 23rd Street, New York 10, New York.

Schulz, Florence, *Worship With Nursery Children.* National Council of Churches of Christ, Office of Publication and Distribution, 120 East 23rd Street, New York 10, New York.

Sherrill, Helen H. and Sherrill, Lewis J., *Interpreting Death to Children.* National Council of Churches of Christ, Office of Publication and Distribution, 120 East 23rd Street, New York 10, New York.

Storms, Grace E., *The Young Child Starts to Church.* National Council of Churches of Christ, Office of Publication and Distribution, 120 East 23rd Street, New York 10, New York.

(Write to your denominational headquarters for information about curriculum and other materials for the three-year-old program in the church and home.)

CHAPTER FOUR

BOOKS

Baruch, Dorothy W., *New Ways of Discipline* (New York: McGraw-Hill Book Co.).

Hymes, James L., Jr., *Behavior and Misbehavior* (New York: Prentice-Hall).

Lee, Irving J., *How to Talk With People* (New York: Harper & Brothers).

PAMPHLETS

Helping Teachers Understand Children. Prepared for the Commission on Teacher Education by the staff of the Division of Child Development and Teacher Personnel. Washington, D. C. American Council on Education.

Wolf, Katherine M., *The Controversial Problem of Discipline.* The Child Study Association of America, 132 East 74th Street, New York 21, New York.

PERIODICALS

Adult Leadership. Adult Education Association of the USA, 743 North Wabash Avenue, Chicago 11, Illinois.

CHAPTER FIVE

BOOKS

Fox, H. W., *The Child's Approach to Religion* (New York: Harper & Brothers).

Jones, Mary Alice, *The Faith of Our Children* (Nashville: Abingdon Press).

Manwell, Elizabeth M. and Fahs, Sophia L., *Consider the Children: How They Grow*, 1st edition revised (Boston: Beacon Press).

Smither, Ethel L., *The Use of the Bible With Children* (Nashville: Abingdon Press).

Whitehouse, Elizabeth S., *Opening the Bible to Children* (St. Louis: The Bethany Press).

PAMPHLETS

Williams, Daniel Day, *Christian Teaching and Christian Beliefs.* The Division of Christian Education, 14 Beacon Street, Boston 8, Massachusetts.

LEAFLETS

Schulz, Florence, *Worship With Nursery Children.* National Council of Churches of Christ, Office of Publication and Distribution, 120 East 23rd Street, New York 10, New York.

Sherrill, Helen H. and Sherrill, Lewis J., *Interpreting Death to Children.* National Council of Churches of Christ, Office of Publication and Distribution, 120 East 23rd Street, New York 10, New York.

CHAPTER SIX

BOOKS

Hiltner, Seward, *Pastoral Counseling* (Nashville: Abingdon Press).
Hymes, James L., Jr., *Understanding Your Child* (New York: Prentice-Hall).
Lee, Irving J., *How to Talk With People* (New York: Harper & Brothers).
Rogers, Carl, *Client-Centered Therapy* (Boston: Houghton Mifflin Co.).
Spock, Benjamin, *Baby and Child Care* (New York: Pocket Books, Inc.).

LEAFLETS

Sherrill, Helen H. and Sherrill, Lewis J., *Interpreting Death to Children*. National Council of Churches of Christ, Office of Publication and Distribution, 120 East 23rd Street, New York 10, New York.
Storms, Grace E., *The Young Child Starts to Church*. National Council of Churches of Christ, Office of Publication and Distribution, 120 East 23rd Street, New York 10, New York.

(See also " General References for Parents " on page 173 of this bibliography.)

CHAPTER SEVEN

LEAFLETS

Burns, Charles L., Jr., *Using Role Playing in Christian Education*. National Council of Churches of Christ, Office of Publication and Distribution, 120 East 23rd Street, New York 10, New York.
Schuman, Claire S. and Tarcov, Oscar, *To Clarify Our Problems: A Guide to Role Playing*. Anti-Defamation League of B'Nai B'Rith, 515 Madison Avenue, New York 22, New York.

CHAPTERS EIGHT AND NINE

BOOKS

Baruch, Dorothy W., *New Ways in Discipline* (New York: McGraw-Hill Book Co.).
Gordon, Thomas, *Group-Centered Leadership* (Boston: Houghton Mifflin Co.).
Howe, Reuel L., *Man's Need and God's Action* (Greenwich: The Seabury Press).
Lee, Irving J., *How to Talk With People* (New York: Harper & Brothers).
Leonard, Edith M.; Vandeman, Dorothy D.; Miles, Lillian E., *Counseling With Parents* (New York: The Macmillan Co.).
May, Rollo, *Man's Search for Himself* (New York: W. W. Norton & Company, Inc.).
Overstreet, Harry A., *The Mature Mind* (New York: W. W. Norton & Company, Inc.).

PAMPHLETS

Mayer, Jane, *Getting Along in the Family*. Parent Teacher Series. Bureau of Publications, Teachers College, Columbia University, New York 27.

LEAFLETS

The Leader's Digest. Articles selected from *Adult Leadership* magazine, Volume No. I. 1952-53. Adult Education Association of the USA, 743 North Wabash Avenue, Chicago 11, Illinois.

PERIODICALS

Adult Leadership. Adult Education Association of the USA, 743 North Wabash Avenue, Chicago 11, Illinois.

Chapter Ten

BOOKS

Abingdon Bible Commentary (Nashville: Abingdon Press).

Baillie, John, *The Daily Practice of Prayer* (New York: Charles Scribner's Sons).

———, *Diary of Private Prayer* (New York: Charles Scribner's Sons).

Day, Albert E., *An Autobiography of Prayer* (New York: Harper & Brothers).

Fosdick, Harry Emerson, *The Meaning of Prayer* (New York: Association Press).

Hiltner, Seward, *Self-Understanding* (New York: Charles Scribner's Sons).

Interpreter's Bible (Nashville: Abingdon Press).

Liebman, Joshua, *Peace of Mind* (New York: Simon and Schuster, Inc.).

MacMurray, John, *Reason and Emotion* (New York: Barnes & Noble, Inc.).

May, Rollo, *Man's Search for Himself* (New York: W. W. Norton & Company, Inc.).

Micklem, Nathaniel, *Ultimate Questions* (Nashville: Abingdon Press).

Miller, Samuel, *Great Realities* (New York: Harper & Brothers).

———, *The Life of the Soul* (New York: Harper & Brothers).

Overstreet, Harry A., *The Mature Mind* (New York: W. W. Norton & Company, Inc.).

Steere, Douglas, *Time to Spare* (New York: Harper & Brothers).

Trueblood, Elton, *Alternative to Futility* (New York: Harper & Brothers).

Chapter Eleven

BOOKS

MacMurray, John, *Reason and Emotion* (New York: Barnes & Noble).

Mitchell, Lucy Sprague (ed.), *Another Here and Now Story Book* (New York: E. P. Dutton & Co., Inc.).

Ribble, Margaret A., *The Rights of Infants* (New York: Columbia University Press).

(Write to your denominational headquarters for information about curriculum and other materials for use with two-year-olds, toddlers, and babies in the church and home.)

CHAPTER TWELVE

BOOKS

Foster, Josephine C. and Mattson, Marion L., *Nursery School Education* (New York: Appleton-Century-Crofts, Inc.).

Read, Katherine H., *The Nursery School: A Human Relationships Laboratory* (Philadelphia: W. B. Saunders Co.).

PAMPHLETS

Conover, E. M., *The Church School and Parish House Building*. National Council of Churches of Christ, Office of Publication and Distribution, 120 East 23rd Street, New York 10, New York.

Equipment and Supplies. Association for Childhood Education International, 1200 15th Street, N. W., Washington 5, D. C.

LEAFLETS

Campbell, Elizabeth, *Nursery Children Play at Church*. National Council of Churches of Christ, Office of Publication and Distribution, 120 East 23rd Street, New York 10, New York.

The Church's Ministry to Nursery Children and Their Family. National Council of Churches of Christ, Office of Publication and Distribution, 120 East 23rd Street, New York 10, New York. Write for information about available titles in this series.

Nicolaysen, Mary, *Art Activities in the Nursery Program*. National Council of Churches of Christ, Office of Publication and Distribution, 120 East 23rd Street, New York 10, New York.

Portfolio for Nursery School Teachers. The Association for Childhood Education International, 1200 15th Street, N. W., Washington 5, D. C.

(Write to your denominational headquarters for information about program and other materials for through-the-week nursery schools.)